Guerilla Garage Sales:

Boot Camp for the Beginner

As Told by a Global Tactical Guerilla Specialist

CA$H HOFFMAN

PublishAmerica
Baltimore

© 2006 by Cash Hoffman.
All rights reserved. No part of this book may be reproduced, stored in a retrieval system or transmitted in any form or by any means without the prior written permission of the publishers, except by a reviewer who may quote brief passages in a review to be printed in a newspaper, magazine or journal.

First printing

At the specific preference of the author, PublishAmerica allowed this work to remain exactly as the author intended, verbatim, without editorial input.

ISBN: 1-4241-3523-0
PUBLISHED BY PUBLISHAMERICA, LLLP
www.publishamerica.com
Baltimore

Printed in the United States of America

DEDICATION

This is in honor of the United States Army, Navy, Air Force, Marine Corps, and all of the brave men and women in uniform who made this book and our American way of life possible. Without their supreme sacrifice and steadfast devotion to our country's security and protection, we would not have the freedom to enjoy life and the pursuit of happiness that we often take for granted. We salute them for what they do, so we can do what we do.

ACKNOWLEDGEMENT

I would like to express my gratitude to a number of people who encouraged me to write this book. I would like to thank Nick and Yvonne Bledsoe, who introduced me to eBay, and David Wooddell for his technical computer support. I also want to thank my number one supporters, my family—my father and Grandpa Moon who taught me the value of a dollar—my mom who knows where to find everything in the world—and my brother Stephen, who set very high standards of achievement. I really want to thank all the people at Publish America who made my dream a reality.

FOREWORD

As a nation, we have come of age through technology. Internet technology is empowering entrepreneurs like Austin Hoffman to operate their own online businesses. When I first met this young man in January 2004, he was a winner of the TCU Youth Entrepreneur of the Year award and a sophomore in high school. Already a veteran of hundreds of garage sales, auctions, and flea markets, Austin was well on his way at an early age. Unlike most books on this topic which tend to concentrate on computer application, *Guerilla Garage Sales* is filled with sound business principles, plus helpful tips on how to operate a small business and product acquisition. Ranging from real-life business experiences to the imaginative weaving of historical events, Austin's how-to approach appeals to a wide range of ages and walks of life. Written in a clear, direct style, this is an indispensable guide for anyone not familiar with the brave new world of online store operation. This little guide will bring you hours of thought provoking, useful, and memorable rules for selling on the Net.

Randy Eisenman
CEO & President
Handango

TABLE OF CONTENTS

SECTION ONE: ACQUIRING AND EVALUATING INVENTORY..17

I. The First Garage Sale—Introduction to "Guerilla" Garage Sales..17

II. The First Raid—How to begin—basic equipment and organizing an online business......................................19

III. Target Garage Sales—Introduction to purchasing inventory at Garage Sales..25

> *Rule No. 1 Uniform of the Day—Dress and appearance attending garage sales*

> *Rule No. 2 Deal with the Female Station Chief— How to interact with garage sale hosts*

> *Rule No. 3 Buy in Bulk for the Convoy—The most expeditious way to acquire inventory at a garage sale*

> *Rule No. 4 Deploy when the Quartermaster is Busy—How to conduct yourself and exit garage sales*

> *Rule No. 5 Have Correct Currency in Country— Best way to pay for garage sale purchases*

Rule No. 6 Negotiate from a Position of Strength—How to haggle and get the best price at garage sales, and when not to dicker

Rule No. 7 Command and Control—Basic psychology of garage sales and how to use it to your advantage

Rule No. 8 Do Not Let Your Guard Down on Station—How to subvert your true agenda

Rule No. 9 Be Prepared for Any Contingency—Time management and the importance of details

Rule No. 10 Have the Patience of a Forward Observer—Business discipline in acquiring inventory and how to minimize losses

Rule No. 11 Network the Trail—How to deal with competitors and rivals to your advantage

Rule No. 12 Store Up for the Monsoon—Buying and selling seasonal merchandise

Rule No. 13 Battle Plan: Map a Plan of Attack—How to prepare an effective garage sale itinerary

Rule No. 14 Recon/Go Early, Go Back, Go Beyond—The importance of timing in business

Rule No. 15 Utilize All Resources at Your Disposal—How to attack garage sales like a guerilla—get in and get out, with a minimum of effort and expense.

Rule No. 16 Newly Issued Stores—When to automatically purchase certain products at garage sales

Rule No. 17 Landmines to Avoid on Bivouac and in the Field—Checklist of common mistakes to avoid

IV. Operation Auction—How to conduct yourself at traditional auctions..49

V. Interdict Estate Sales—Attending estate sales to acquire merchandise...57

VI. Massing Materiel—Finding wholesale markets and other sources of inventory for your business.........................59

VII. Know Your Arsenal—Marketing your business effectively to reach your target audience................................63

VIII. KP Detail—Touch-up and cleaning of merchandise to maximize its condition and value.....................................67

IX. Intelligence Gathering—How to properly grade your purchases for sale on the Internet......................................72

X. The Most Common SNAFU—Avoiding the *Mint Condition* trap...80

SECTION TWO: OPERATING YOUR BUSINESS EFFICIENTLY AND GOOD RECORD KEEPING.......................................81

I.   Time is of the Essence—Importance of time management and valuing your time..................................81

II.   Condition, Condition, Condition—Goodwill and valuing your products...83

III.   Purchase for Your Own HQ—How to increase profits by purchasing supplies and equipment for your own account...85

IV.   Be All You Can Be—Need for business specialization...86

V.   Recycle and Live Off the Land—Making additional income and protecting the environment at the same time...89

VI.   Protect Your Force—Evaluating risk and increasing revenues via self-insurance.......................................91

VII.   Assessment and Command Information—Pricing your goods and services in a highly competitive market...93

VIII.   Kill Them with Kindness—The crux of good service and the value of a customer.....................................100

IX.   Maximize Your Communications Array—Importance of customer communication and avoiding problems with customers...103

X.   Define Your Mission—Why you should have a mission statement and how to practically relate it to your business...106

XI.   Retain Government Records in Triplicate—Business record keeping and information retrieval........110

XII.   Uncle Sam Needs You—Basic information on maintaining business tax records and tax preparation....117

XIII.   Photo Reconnaissance—Using a camera in your online business to target your market...........................120

XIV.   Logistical Support—Packing your orders like a pro..130

XV.   Splitting Your Force—Marketing and selling products on consignment...142

SECTION THREE: THE ELECTRONIC AD AND SELLING ON THE INTERNET..149

I. Getting from the Flea Market to the Internet— Introduction to online selling, writing and designing ads, producing and listing ads, and how to use several common platforms to market your products...................................151

II. In the Beginning—Try eBay....................................153

      Step 1: Registering on eBay

      Step 2: Becoming ID Verified

III. Navigating the eBay Website...................................155

IV. Research on eBay..161

      Step 1: Pricing payoff

      Step 2: Survey Completed Items

V. Sell Your Item on eBay..166

      Step 1: Choosing a Category

      Step 2: Creating Ad Title and Item Specifics

      Step 3: Ad Composition

      Step 4: Creating an Ad Template

Step 5: Payment and Shipping Conditions

Step 6: Timing Your Ad For Best Results

VI.   Registering on PayPal.........................179

Part 1: What is PayPal?

Part 2: Why Would a Seller Accept PayPal?

Part 3: How Does PayPal Work?

Part 4: How Secure is PayPal?

Part 5: Papal Pros and Cons

Part 6: Other Online "Banking" Companies

Part 7: PayPal Fees

Part 8: PayPal is Here to Stay

Part 9: Installing a PayPal Account

VII: Navigating the PayPal Website.........................188

VIII: Second Front—The "Half Track" in Combat—
Utilizing Half.Com to market your goods.....................192

IX: How To Sell on Half.Com...................195

Step 1: Become a Member

Step 2: Create a Seller's Account

Step 3: Sell Your Stuff

Step 4: Completing the Sale

Step 5: Shipping Considerations

Step 6: Half.Com's Commission

Step 7: Half.Com's Condition Policy

Step 8: Half's Positives

Step 9: Half's Negatives

X.   Photo Intelligence – Maximizing your photographic presence on the web and minimizing cost by hosting your own pictures..209

XI.   Chatter—The importance of eBay Feedback and other acclaim between you and customers—good and bad...212

XII.   Safe Harbor—Guidelines for avoiding online fraud and sanctions from customers and web hosts..................220

XIII.   Strategic Wild Card—Conclusion and challenge...232

XIV.   Glossary of Terms..233

SECTION ONE

ACQUIRING AND EVALUATING INVENTORY

I. THE FIRST GARAGE SALE

No one knows when the first garage sale was held. Its origins are lost in antiquity. Of course it would be safe to assume the precepts date back much farther than introduction of the garage. As popular legend has it, one of the first such events in recorded history occurred when Marcus Aurelius, Emperor of Rome in A.D.169, needed to raise revenue to repulse Germanic tribes threatening the empire from the north. Because of the immediate threat this posed, and lack of time to collect tax revenue from the populace, for several months he held a "royal" garage sale in the palace to raise money for his legions by selling many of his imperial possessions and those of his wife, Faustina.

At the age of 14, I went to my first garage sale. The night before this momentous occasion, I asked my father what to expect. He said it would be like "guerilla warfare." I thought this was an odd statement at the time, but now, after five years (and counting) of "attacking" hundreds of them, I know what he meant. Although my father sometimes has a penchant for being overly dramatic, going to garage sales for the serious minded entrepreneur has many parallels to that distinct form of unconventional warfare. You get up at first light after carefully mapping and plotting a detailed route and plan of attack. You wear drab, nondescript clothing and camouflage your appearance to avoid sticking out in a crowd. Like a soldier serving in military conflict, you develop a discipline and manner of operation and employ specialized equipment, terminology, and techniques for each assault. You

17

CASH HOFFMAN

insert your unit in small numbers into as many garages, yards, storage units, flea markets, and parking lots as you possibly can in the shortest time span, hopefully in advance of any opposing forces, and then repel into the countryside, only to come back to "attack" again, to garage sale another day—with the same objective repeated over and over again.

II

YOUR FIRST RAID

You are going to be a tactical guerilla specialist. You are going to be able to secure the inventory you need to operate your business. You are going to acquire numerous skills and tools to compete with anyone at any level of business you choose. You are going to move ahead of the competition and have every possible advantage in your pursuits. You will keep your eyes and ears open your mind alert at all times, and always be on your toes. You will become disciplined and expert at your job. Whether or not you succeed will depend on how much better you are at your job than your competition. It will come down to which unit implements its directive best, and integrates them with good management practices. That is a large order, but if you give the best that is in you, you will succeed. You will become a *tactical guerilla specialist.* In "The Millionaire Next Door" Thomas J. Stanley and William Danko researched how individuals acquire wealth: "Why do people operate their own businesses? First, most successful business owners will tell you that they have tremendous freedom. They are their own bosses. Also, they tell us that self-employment is less risky than working for others.

A professor once asked a group of sixty MBA students who were executives of public corporations this question:

What is risk?
One student replied:
Being an entrepreneur!

His fellow students agreed. Then the professor answered his own question with a quote from an entrepreneur:

*What is risk? Having one source of income. Employees are at risk…
They have a single source of income. What about the entrepreneur who
sells janitorial services to your employers? He has hundreds and
hundreds of customers…hundreds and hundreds of sources of
income."*

What you need to start your business income stream will vary depending upon your intended level of operation, and what area of merchandising and products you choose to sell. Obviously you will need a reliable computer with Internet access, and transportation for reconnoitering the various sales each week. As for me, I had an adequate personal computer, an inexpensive digital camera, and $200.00. That was all I needed to begin this exciting business. As far as business startup costs go, this was a trivial amount. Can you name any other business that you can begin with such a meager investment? Can you think of any other business venture with very little risk and millions of potential customers? How many business opportunities legitimately allow you to start part time, and when you decide to go full time, make a good living without leaving your home? How else could you make money while you sleep? The amount of time you spend is strictly up to you. You can increase or decrease your level of involvement whenever you choose. According to Entrepreneur Magazine, the average franchise cost today is $70,000.00, and that only covers the franchise business certificate. That does not include a place to operate your business, equipment, furniture, supplies, fixtures, insurance, operating capital or anything else. In my view, an Internet business is not work, it is entertaining and just plain fun! And you don't have to go to work to get to work. Because I did not have a driver's license, my dad had to chauffeur me for the first two and a half years of combat. During my first year, I purchased: a vehicle that I customized as a special purpose transport for my business; an electronic scale; a better digital camera; seven bookcases; a deskjet printer; a supply cabinet; a library cart; and storage cabinets for inventory. Adequate storage is an extremely important requirement. If you have access to a warehouse, hangar, or storage building you will be ahead of the game, because you can fill up the HQ with garage sale items very quickly. I have very tolerant parents, but most of my business conflicts developed not with my customers, but with my mother. My mom often contended that I was filling up her house with junk and she was going to get rid of it if I did not get it out of her living room. I told her it was not junk, it was inventory, but she was not impressed—you know how mothers are. I may bivouac there, but this was her headquarters and base of operations.

Depending on where you headquarter, there are several logistical prerequisites to make ready in order to reach full combat readiness:

A: If you need start up capital, contact the Small Business Administration, a branch of the United States Government. In business, it is all about capital, networking, and marketing. If you are starting a new business, remember, like the Titanic, most new businesses fail during their first year of operation. Furthermore, I must point out that the Titanic was constructed, launched, and operated by professionals. According to the Small Business Administration about half a million small businesses close up shop every year. The number one reason for business failure is undercapitalization. When it comes to capital there never seems to be enough.

B: Some state and local governments may require permits or other application to do business in your jurisdiction. Before you begin business, you need to research and make contact with: state and local governmental agencies regulating business in your area; libraries, attorneys, accountants, and other professionals; local chambers of commerce; colleges and other schools; trade and industrial associations.

C: Contact your state tax agency for guidance on state income tax compliance, and the Internal Revenue Service for federal tax guidelines.

D: Apply for a Federal Identification Number with Internal Revenue Service, if you are going to do business under any name or entity other than your own name and your own Social Security Number. You can file electronically on the IRS web site (referenced later on in this book) to secure the proper federal identification.

E: File your business name selection in the assumed name records (usually the courthouse) where you live if you are going to use a business name that differs from your own. You must register your assumed name where you reside and where you do business. Often referred to as a d.b.a. (doing business as), in Texas the filing will be maintained for ten years before you have to renew the certificate. If you fail to comply with this registration process and record this election in advance, you cannot operate under an assumed name, and financial institutions will not allow you to open an account. Failure to file could result in legal penalty, someone else could officially appropriate your business name, and you might not have any recourse. According to the Uniform Commercial Code, some states require initial public notification such as publishing your d.b.a. in the newspaper or other public places.

F: Learn whether or not you have to collect sales tax. Contact the state agency regulating sales taxes.

G: Set up a bank account for each business entity you intend to operate. Only deposit funds and write checks on the account pertaining to that specific business. *NEVER* write personal checks on the account or conduct personal business from the account—*EVER!*

H: Open a PayPal account (Section Three).

I: If you plan to have employees, find out what records you have to keep for each state, local, and federal agency.

J: Hire an accountant or bookkeeper and set up your books, or purchase software for this purpose.

K: You generally need a credit card for most e-business sites, but some will accept a bank account or a debit card.

L: To succeed in business you need a presence on the Web. Register a domain name at www.*netnation.com* (call toll free 1-888-277-0000), www.*domainpeople.com* (call toll free 1-877-831—2562), or find another registrar at *Icann.org*. Choose a catchy name that identifies what you do, personifies your business, and is available. If possible, try to pick a name with class and distinction the public will remember and associate with your operation, but keep it simple. Many domain possibilities exist. Millions of names have already been chosen by other businesses. "Cybersquatters" have gobbled up countless others to sell for a premium to end-users like us. Choose a name that is short and memorable so people can remember it, like a telephone number. If possible purchase multiple names covering your business, your products, or to avoid customer confusion with other

GUERILLA GARAGE SALES

businesses. Additional domain names could steer business to you when people do not know your correct name or site. Avoid weird spellings or hyphenation, which could adversely affect traffic. The cost is usually $30 a year to register a new domain name. Most providers accept discounts for multiple years, up to ten years in advance. Registration sites provide assistance in choosing a name, or locating and purchasing one that is already registered.

M: Get an e-mail address from an Internet Service Provider.

N: If you are concerned about your address being published on the Net, consider a Post Office box or drop box.

O: If you are not 18 years old you cannot do business by yourself. Everything will have to be conducted in the name of an adult, such as a parent or guardian. In the beginning I had to do business in my Dad's name, but I wasn't just using my Dad's name to get business. I wanted to earn it.

P: Invest in auction software to save time by automating many of the details of daily operation like ad preparation and design, notifying buyers at the end of auction, and assistance with other information services.

Q: You may want a separate telephone number to avoid business calls to your home. Depending on your type of business and anticipated calling volume, research a toll free telephone number.

R: Buy some inexpensive mailing labels that contain your business address and e-mail address.

S: Check out websites selling products you are considering for your business. Find the hot items and the popular categories. Study ad copy, pictures, and layout of the ads. Look at completed items to determine if the item sold and the final sales price. Absorb as much information as you can from the "HELP" sections on multiple sites. This will educate you on the rules of operation, what to do to avoid complications, and how to handle problems before they occur.

23

T: Before you begin selling, buy something online for yourself or your business. This will familiarize you with the auction process and hopefully make you a better seller, because you will have a first hand knowledge of what a buyer experiences on the Internet.

U: Before you do anything else, sell some items you already own. This is an inexpensive way to begin. You will have nothing invested in the merchandise and you can get a feel for the process before you make a serious commitment.

V: Devise a budget and keep to it. If you cannot pay cash do not buy it.

W: Learn all you can about the products you sell.

X: Stay trained and current on shipping regulations.

Y: Know your limitations and never promise what you cannot deliver.

Z: No matter the size, vow to improve something associated with your business every day.

III

TARGET GARAGE SALES

Although I will brief you on auctions and other types of merchandise buying later on, the staple for most people who want to make extra money on the World Wide Web is the typical American garage sale. Sometimes called a *yard sale* or *rummage sale*, it is a relatively inexpensive form of commerce that almost anyone can master, following graduation from guerilla Internet boot camp. As a global tactical guerilla specialist, on average I spend about two hours a day on my business and earn about $200 a week. There are two types of garage sales—those designed to make money or those just to get rid of stuff. You need to be able to tell the difference in the first five minutes of every engagement. The average garage sale is a commonplace event, usually held on a weekend, and is most often utilized by people in your community to clean out attics, closets, basements, and other areas of their homes. It is also a fundraising tool for local churches, charities, schools, and other organizations. Basically, people are getting rid of their unwanted items and their loss can be your gain. It is like army surplus. They no longer have an emotional attachment to this property. It may be that the item in question is brand new, still contained in the original packaging, and has never been opened. I have not taken psychology in high school yet, so I cannot give you a professional or scientific reason, but I know from experience that you need to focus on this single aspect of the equation—they want to get rid of it!

All you have to do is convince the seller that you are willing to take this item off their hands, but you do not want to spend a lot of time or money doing it. Now, I would never tell anyone to lie or stretch the truth, but the absolute fact of the matter is this: if you are totally forthcoming at the "point of purchase", as they say in marketing, you will not be very successful. If, for example, you tell the seller at the garage sale that you make a living on the

25

internet, that you want this expensive piece of Noritake china that he has for sale, you came here specifically to buy this item, and that you intend to re-sell it for handsome profit on *e-Bay*, what do you think would happen? If he did not quote you a very high price for the china, the seller might just keep the item and not sell it at all. In fact, on more than one occasion I have had sellers take items from my hands and say they no longer wanted to sell them, when they came to their senses and suddenly realized what they had. Believe it or not, just like a military campaign, there are unwritten rules of engagement in this quasi-combat civilian enterprise that the experts know, that I have learned through experience. And I want to dispatch them to you—in the order of appearance, not necessarily importance.

RULE NO. 1 UNIFORM OF THE DAY

What is the dress protocol? Is there a special type of attire or image that you want to project in this business? First of all from a tactical standpoint, unlike most civilian undertakings, I do not necessarily put my best foot forward. Various authors over the years have successfully sold a lot of books and merchandise that stand for the proposition that you should "dress for success" and "clothes make the man." I take the flip side of that successful clothing philosophy and apply it to my garage sale business. But more importantly, if I have an overarching bias, it is toward pragmatism. I do not exactly look like a street person when I garage sale, but I definitely dress down to camouflage my strategic initiative. I do not believe that you can make good buys in this field of endeavor if you drive up to the seller's yard in a brand new Humvee, wearing your dress uniform, and flash a lot of cash. I even go so far as to *not* incorporate anything on my person remotely "controversial" in my clothing or appearance. The reason for this is you never know what may turn someone off—tattoos, body piercing, weird hair, tobacco and liquor advertising, sports teams, controversial slogans, products, brands, hunting, gun products, advertising, slogans, etc. I wear very plain clothes in earth tone colors such as blue jeans, and a nondescript cap. I am always clean, without sunglasses, cigarettes, or other tobacco products. I never wear jewelry, not even my dog tags, or other accessories, and my billfold and coin pouch are low budget "Government Issue." I am polite, I make eye contact with the seller, and I initiate a polite, friendly comment when I approach the sale to develop a rapport with the host. Pursuing your objective is like shooting in a battlefield of moving targets. Every time you hit one, two more pop up from another direction.

RULE NO. 2 DEAL WITH THE FEMALE STATION CHIEF

Even though a sale might be conducted by a husband and wife team, as a young man, and a prospective buyer, if I want to make the best deal when I am behind the lines, I usually seek out the woman in charge to ask my questions when I am ready to check out. I cannot give you a scientific reason and I am not a male chauvinist, but women are generally easier to deal with at garage sales. In our country, it is a well-known societal fact that women do most of the shopping. They handle the household effects significantly more often than do men. And, they usually have to dispose of the leftover property if it does not sell. At this level they are the least emotionally attached from a monetary and practical standpoint to the garage sale merchandise. Also women are more receptive to change when it comes to redecorating. Women routinely get rid of things to bring in newer items and change the look of the married quarters. Men as a rule are breadwinners, more concerned with price, and from my experience usually more difficult sellers. Men are often more utilitarian. If it works, why fix it—why sell it? I could probably write an entire chapter about the difference between men and women, but that is not the purpose of this exercise. There are always exceptions to any rule in this book, but in general, I have found this to be true. Moreover, I do not blindly follow this rule. While I am looking at each sale, whenever possible I try to observe individual sellers as they interact with other customers before I try making my purchase. Thus, I may modify the rule at any given sale. This is especially true when there is more than one woman in charge at the sale or the host is male. Reaching your goal is a process not an event. It all fits together.

RULE NO. 3 BUY IN BULK FOR THE CONVOY

Do not piecemeal your purchases. I have found from experience that I can acquire more inventory at lower prices by making an offer on multiple items, as opposed to individual purchases at the same sale. I may group all kinds of items together like books, household products, clothing, etc. Also piecemeal buying takes time; and time is money. There is another reason for this rule. If you approach a seller with only one item in your hand, you are obviously interested in this particular item, and the seller may charge more. Whereas if you have several items your intent is somewhat disguised, and it may not be readily apparent which item you are *really* interested in purchasing. If the seller counters, you may put back some items but still end up with the item(s) you really wanted, at the price you originally expected to pay. Or you may pick up several items and find the seller will include them for the same asking price. I know this sounds a little convoluted, but I guarantee you the concept works. Frequently, I just make the following offer:

"Would you take "x"dollars for this?" And I hold out my stack of potential purchases.

Most people just want to get rid of things and usually say yes. When I group my purchases together, I usually pile them in reverse order with the least attractive, most invaluable items at the top. I do not hide items or mislead the seller by indicating incorrect quantities in my group. If asked, I am always truthful. Usually, however, the seller does not take items from me or examine them, but merely accepts my offer of "x"dollars with little fanfare—and I am off to the next waypoint. There is another device that I use when there are only a few items I definitely want to purchase. Often I throw in other merchandise that interests me which may have some value, but about which I am not exactly certain. If I am going to spend the same money for my purchases, it makes sense to get as much as possible for the money. Quite often these "flyers" prove to be more valuable that the original item intended for purchase in the first place. You can never be too ready. The best day is the day ahead.

RULE NO. 4 DEPLOY WHEN THE QUARTERMASTER IS BUSY

In order to successfully complete your purchase, there is one additional tool to remember. Whenever possible, attempt to check out when the seller is busy with other customers. Believe it or not, they are less likely to inspect your stack of purchases or charge you more at this particular time. I walk up, display my stack of items, indicate I am in a hurry, and ask would they take "x" dollars? I also have exact change and tender the cash in the seller's direction. This tactic is most effective when there are people behind you with large stacks of purchases or higher-priced items. The seller will make a quick sale with you to get to the bigger fish. Often they accept my offer without calculating the charges or making a counter-offer, and I am off to the next map coordinate! You do not want to kill a fly with a howitzer!

RULE NO. 5 HAVE CORRECT CURRENCY IN COUNTRY

Before I go to any garage sale, besides having a full fuel tank, I have an ammo-can pre-stocked with currency of all denominations, plus a large number of coins which I keep in my vehicle. I put a small amount of money in my pocket before I approach each sale and stow the rest. I do this for three reasons. First, you will be unsuccessful in your attempt to buy low if you tell someone you only want to pay $5.00 because that is all you can afford, then when you check out you are forced to hand them a twenty dollar bill. Or, it ruins your presentation of lack of funds when you open your wallet to pay and it is full of folding money. Secondly, it saves time if you have correct change; and time is money. Finally, I have sometimes received even lower prices when the seller was not prepared for the sale by having correct change, and in order to conclude the transaction, he accepted less than his asking price. I have often noticed that sellers can overlook the importance of stocking sufficient change before garage sale day, and they will accept a lower offer simply to secure change. Having the right change can be a definite all around advantage and time saver. Also, people are more easily swayed into taking a one dollar price offer, if they do not have to make change. You can never be too ready when you are on point in the forward area.

RULE NO. 6 NEGOTIATE FROM A POSITION OF STRENGTH

This is a direct order from headquarters! NEVER PAY THE ASKING PRICE! I always assume that the stated price is negotiable. Besides offering a smaller amount, I often ask:
"Will you take less on this?", or "Is this your best price?"
If they are offended or fail to budge on their prices, move on quickly to another combat area; you are wasting your time at this waypoint. If you are tactful you can point out that perhaps the condition of the item does not warrant their asking price, but do not insult the merchandise. I ignore every sticker price no matter how it is marked on an item. If you can live with the stated asking price and you feel that you can still make a reasonable profit on the resale, then you may disregard this rule. The only other time I have not followed this rule is when I am about to make a really good buy because the Seller did not know what he had. For example, on one occasion I found a Royal Doulton Toby Mug worth approximately fifty dollars, but it was

marked two dollars. My natural inclination (because I hate to pay the asking price) was to ask the seller if he would take a dollar. Two things stopped me from this course of action. First, reducing this item by one dollar was a stretch, which bothered my conscience since I was already going to make a killing on this transaction. Secondly, there were many other buyers milling around, and if I attempted to negotiate this item, one of them could jump in and start a bidding war. So, the moral of the story is not to get greedy, and of course, realize there is an exception to nearly every rule.

There is another side of Rule No. 6. Do not bid what you think the Seller will accept; and always make your first bid a very low bid. You may be surprised how many times the seller accepts your first offer. Most people who hold garage sales know what to expect and are not insulted with a meager first offer. They anticipate the timeworn process of negotiation. They also understand there are a limited number of buyers who attend garage sales. Furthermore, they realize typically they are not going to get a large number of offers for their belongings; therefore, they are inclined to accept the first offer because they might not get another. Secondly, it is always best to get the seller to tell you his price first. When responding start with a low counteroffer so you will have a lot of room to negotiate. If your first offer is not accepted, most motivated sellers are even more likely to accept your second higher bid (if necessary) to make a sale. Some Sellers deliberately mark up their prices in advance because they expect buyers to haggle with them. Do not think twice about asking for the price of unmarked items because you do not have to buy, just because you ask for a quote. If the seller quotes a high price, reply that you are not interested at that price. The seller might voluntarily reduce the price. If not, you may want to make an offer. Sometimes if you put an item down and act like you are leaving, the seller, fearing no sale, may jump back in and accept your offer, or counteroffer with a more reasonable price. Occasionally if I am trying to buy an item I really want, I tell the seller I am going to my vehicle to borrow some money from my buddy, and often times they accept a lesser offer when I return with my final bid and state:

"This is all I have."

Also, do not appear over-anxious or ask a lot of pricing questions. Sellers often gauge pricing based upon the amount of interest displayed by potential buyers. Finally, it is best to negotiate out of the earshot of other buyers if you are trying to make a deal. The Seller is more likely to work with you but without an audience. It is not an either/or situation. Learn the art of negotiation; there are good buys and there are better buys. Find out what works for you and follow these guidelines faithfully until they become second nature to you. Begin; the rest is easy.

RULE NO. 7 COMMAND AND CONTROL

Remember when I said earlier that the sellers are probably no longer emotionally attached to their belongings once they stack it in their garages for sale? That may be true, but I have found that most people, for some reason, feel better or exhibit a basic need to sell their belongings to someone who will use it, or provide it with a good home. This can take several forms. Since I am an adolescent, most sellers are comfortable selling items to me they believe a person of my age and sensibilities would normally use or purchase, such as books, videos, CDs, clothing, games, and even toys. In fact, I am usually able to buy those items at a very good price because, more often than not, the seller wants to impart them to me. And it makes him or her feel good about my purchasing their property. Another point to consider is charitable and other third party sales. In such instances, someone other than the original owner is selling goods. These people are usually even less emotionally connected to sales items at this juncture, allowing me to make even better buys. Pay strict attention though. If the check-out person or sales attendant on the floor has personal knowledge of the item I am buying, he probably donated it and may remain emotionally bonded to it. What would a seller think if I walked up to the checkout table with a Barbie dollhouse? In fact, sellers have asked me:

"What are you going to do with that [item]?"

I usually try to anticipate what a seller may ask me ahead of time so I do not appear to be totally outside my character and less than forthcoming in my response. Therefore, when I am buying other items that one would not normally associate with a person of my age, I volunteer statements to the effect that my family or someone in my family may have a use for the item, which makes the seller more receptive to my offer. In the final analyses, I guess it is human nature to desire that their possessions end up in a good home or may be useful to other people. Nonetheless, this is a technique that I use to my advantage and your mission is to push yourself to the edge of your talent. It is going to be an all out war.

RULE NO. 8 DO NOT LET DOWN YOUR GUARD ON STATION

I try to be consistent in appearance, purchases, and actions and not to stick out in the crowd or draw attention to myself. We soldiers must submerge our true agenda. Appear to be a casual garage sale buyer, not a veteran weekend warrior. Make the purchase as soon as possible or leave for the next rendezvous point. When approaching the seller for checkout, make mundane statements about the items you are purchasing such as, "This bowl would look great on my mother's table," and "My grandfather works in the motor pool. He has a Jeep and I think he could use this repair manual," will reinforce your purchase. Do not profess to have any expertise in the area of the purchase or indicate that you collect the purchase items. These are tip-offs to sellers that they may be dealing with a pro, which can cost you monetarily. On occasion I may not want to let the seller know what I am trying to find. At such times, when quizzed by the seller, I merely say:

"I don't know what I'm looking for, but when I see it I'll know it."

They usually leave me alone after that. Often when I walk up to a sale and they ask me what a young man like me is doing out so early in the morning, I usually reply jokingly:

"I don't have a life and I'm looking for a bargain because my allowance is so small."

In the end the imitators will fall to the real thing.

RULE NO. 9 BE PREPARED FOR ANY CONTINGENCY

The Boy Scouts of America do not own the franchise on this concept. I was a Boy Scout once, and this cardinal rule of scouting is just as applicable to the garage sale business. The gist of this rule is that I take care of *all* details prior to the morning of the sale. I make certain that my transport has plenty of gas, that I have sufficient currency in all denominations in my ammo-can, that my itinerary has been completely prepared and printed, and there is nothing remaining to be done. I even pick out my attire for the next day and have suitable rations prepared for the upcoming mission to save time. I think that the reason for taking care of these details is obvious; nevertheless, many people are not prepared. Furthermore, as I continue to point out, *Time is money*! If on the day of the sale you have to stop for gasoline or change or food, you could arrive at a good sale too late and miss the opportunity to acquire a good buy. When I was a raw recruit, I walked up on more than one sale and watched the enemy intercept my objective, quickly withdrawing with a cache of items that I wanted, and only one minute of time separated us. However, following the proven guidelines in this manual will help you be more successful and complete your objectives without interference from your adversary. Adherence to this rule is the key. *Always being prepared* also means being flexible and inventive. If I attend a sale, and the seller comes to the door and says that he is not open yet, do I simply accept my fate and say:

"Thank you, I'll come back later."

Or, do I take the initiative:

"I have to go to my brother's birthday party later and I can't come back. Do you by chance have any books or videos for sale?"

If it is raining or snowing do I stay home, or do I go out and make even better buys because the majority of my competition is at home? Another tactic is to even help sellers unpack or move things into their driveway to speed up the opening. Preparation means carrying a flashlight to properly identify street and house numbers and merchandise and taking plastic grocery bags, newspapers, old towels, and boxes to each sale to wrap and protect items. It would be a tragedy to make a good buy and then lose it because it was not protected during combat operations. Protect metal, plastic, wood, and more durable items also. They can be dented and damaged almost as easily as glassware. Finally, you have only a finite amount of time to complete the mission. Maximize it, use it to your advantage, and be prepared to deal with unanticipated things that often happen. A famous general once remarked, "The army that gets there first with the most wins." *Carpe diem every day!*

RULE NO. 10 HAVE THE PATIENCE OF A FORWARD OBSERVER

Patience has so many rewards. This is not an exercise where you always fire your weapon and get a medal. There are periods of time when I fail to purchase inventory because the quality or the price is not satisfactory. On the first day I began my garage sale business, I visited over ten locations and bought only six Norman Rockwell coffee mugs at one sale, because the price was right. That was the extent of my purchases for the entire first week of operation. It was a meager beginning, but I was taught by the *CO* during my first mission not to have an itchy trigger finger and force a sale. In other words, I do not buy just anything. If it is not a good buy and I cannot resell it for a profit, I do not buy it. On many occasions I find myself late in my itinerary and I have not made a purchase; but through discipline I keep holding out for the right time and place to make worthwhile purchases, which is usually just around the corner.

From a marketing perspective, sometimes items do not sell right away; there may be no good reason other than timing or not enough buyers online during that listing period. Maybe I did not market the item properly, and I needed to consider another angle, like grouping it with similar items. Being patient is never forgetting that you have not exhausted all possibilities. "I have not failed. I've just found 10,000 ways that won't work." *–Thomas Edison.*

For example, there are several big sales in my area I try to attend each year. Although the sale might start at 8:00 a.m., I am usually one of the first people to arrive at the event by as much as two or three hours in advance of the opening, and I wait in line. As a rule, I spend approximately $30.00 a day on purchases and usually amass around $250.00 worth of inventory to re-sell. My philosophy is I MAKE MORE MONEY ON THE ITEMS THAT I DO NOT BUY, rather than on the ones I actually purchase. What I mean by this is that I would be guilty of dereliction of duty if I waste money on things that do not eventually sell and I have to get rid of them. Think of all the wasted time and expense! Sometimes the best decision is not to buy at all. Imprudent buying would be an improper deployment of time and resources for no gain. Remember this directive: *Gain is the name of the game. The reason for being in business is profit, not fame!*

RULE NO. 11 NETWORK THE TRAIL

As I travel the "trail," I will often come in contact with other collectors, dealers, and entrepreneurs much like myself, who specialize in the sale and distribution of all kinds of products. To expand my success I develop a *contact sphere*. This is a group of business professionals who complement each other. Through networking, the group can make the most effective use of the strengths of every individual. Believe it or not, most of the individuals with whom I compete are not necessarily the enemy in this "war." In my experience, the large percentage of people who frequent the same sales I do are usually interested in other things, and in fact are not directly in competition with me. The few competitors that I do have are my rivals and we try to beat each other to the draw at every opportunity. I purposely make a concerted effort to get to know these "indigenous friendlies" who recon garage sales in tandem with me. First, I try to associate each face with their individual specialty. If I know someone is collecting golf clubs, they are probably not a threat to me, since I usually do not handle this line of merchandise. Secondly, I make a point to collect the names, telephone numbers, or e-mail addresses of these other dealers. If I ever come across a golf club that interests me, or other items that are unfamiliar to me, I know what specialist to call to ascertain what I may have and its possible worth. This is a valuable tool in my arsenal, which I utilize to maximize profits and minimize time and effort. I find that most other vendors are friendly and willing to help if I am friendly in return and do not pose a threat to their business. I have had vendors tell me things I need to know about sales they have been to, which I have not yet attended. They sometimes provide other useful intelligence to me, and I reciprocate. One important unwritten rule of garage sale etiquette to remember, however, is when you are at a sale or within earshot of a garage sale host do not recognize another vendor or strike up a conversation with him, even though he may be standing right next to you. This is a big breach of security. No one wants the sponsor of the sale to know he or she is a dealer, because there is a legitimate fear that the cost of doing business will be increased if this intelligence is revealed to unauthorized personnel. Likewise, if a raw recruit overtly recognizes me at a sale, I politely ignore him and then explain later after I leave or if I see him in the future. Networking is a key element in developing effective business relationships. It can enable you to gain support from others to help reach your objective. Know your competition and act accordingly.

RULE NO. 12 STORE UP FOR THE MONSOON

When listing an item for sale online, always consider the time of the year. The rule to follow is: *buy out of season and sell in season*. I am not going to spend a lot of time on this, but we have several holidays and four seasons in this country. There are times during the year when people graduate and celebrate birthdays, Mother's Day, Father's Day, other holidays, and annual special events. Be mindful of these unique and special occasions. The best time to buy a good winter coat is during the summer months, and one of the best times to sell that coat is in December. I bought three Halloween costumes in July for a total of $5.00. I sold them the following September for $20.00 each. When I first started in the business I spent a lot of time analyzing what other sellers were doing successfully on their sites. I made notes, and then developed my own plan of attack and merchandising techniques. A good entrepreneur needs to keep his eyes open and make good buys all year long, but do not hesitate to pick up items "out of season" if they are in good condition and they are marketable. Be certain that you can afford to have capital tied up for a longer period of time; and also be sure that you have the storage space to keep these items until later. The message is clear. Only a lack of imagination and the ability to execute keep the entrepreneur from success. Do not become your own worst enemy. Make things happen!

RULE NO. 13 BATTLEPLAN: MAP A PLAN OF ATTACK

I have always believed that if I do not know where I am going, I will have a difficult time getting there. Any battlefield commander will tell you the success of any mission rests on the tactical battle plan and the team executing it. Another important key to military victory is complete knowledge of the battlefield terrain. Every good soldier trains for battle by traversing obstacle courses in simulated combat conditions. Countless hours are spent on the demolition and firing ranges. Recon, scouting, surveillance, and stealth practice is conducted over and again in preparation of the real thing. Constant briefing and "intel" is conducted in advance of issuance of the ultimate mission orders.

Long before the dogs of war are unleashed, many hours of tedious, painstaking work and simulation are required to assess the data and formulate a plan of action. A good military campaign is the successful marriage of planning and mapping skills.

Another important element of any strategic initiative is the itinerary that must be mapped in preparation of every foray into the garage sale jungle to purchase the life's blood of business: your inventory. You now know that time is of the essence, and you will deploy an economy of force, but there is more to this operation.

Tyler, Texas, the Rose Capitol of the World, is an average sized community under 100,000 inhabitants. Tyler has one daily newspaper. There is also a weekly "throwaway" shopper that is distributed free to the public published every Thursday. Between these two publications I prepare my garage sale itinerary, or "map." Recently, both publications began online coverage, which makes my job even easier. Each reference paper publishes a special section reserved for garage sales. Most sales in our area are typically

GUERILLA GARAGE SALES

conducted on Thursday, Friday, and Saturday of each week, with Sunday occasionally thrown in. Texas is in the heart of the "Bible Belt," and Tyler is the "buckle;" therefore, we rarely conduct business transactions on Sunday.

Prior to attending any sale, I review these publications and highlight everything that initially interests me. After all planning and strategy sessions, I type a complete written agenda itemized by hour and half-hour intervals. On a map sheet I list each address by street name and house number, and I include driving directions to each location. Driving directions are detailed, from memory, or I use a freely available commercial mapping software program, such as *MapQuest, Rand McNally, Google.com/maps*, or *Yahoo Maps*. There are several of these free services available on the Internet; they are quite accurate, and extremely useful. I organize each address to travel as the crow flies i.e., the shortest possible distance in the shortest possible time, factoring in the different time starts:

May 20, 2006

6:00 A.M.
New. Gen. Commun. Cen. – 18774 Hwy. 155 South 2.3 miles *Charity*
New Copeland Church – 22431 CR 182 (off New Haven Road) *Church*

7:00 A.M.
3816 & 3817 Post Oak – RIGHT Silverwood, LEFT Caperton, RIGHT
1407 Woodland Hills – RIGHT Post Oak, LEFT Woodland Hills
509 Pam – LEFT off Loop 323 *Books*
2720 Chilton –LEFT Fair, RIGHT Old Bullard, LEFT Chilton

8:00 A.M.
701 Hampton Drive – LEFT Barbee, LEFT Sutherland, RIGHT Hampton
1014 Jeffery Drive – Off Robert E/ Lee *Videos*
9241 Elm – LEFT Cumberland, RIGHT Hickory, LEFT Elm
522 Limerick – RIGHT Dublin, LEFT Limerick

8:30 A.M.
425 Brigadoon – LEFT off Limerick
10817 Chickasha – Old Jackson. 3.3 miles, LEFT Chickasha
1524 Timber Creek—LEFT off Shiloh *Books*
513 W. 5TH – LEFT off Broadway *X-Box*

9:00 A.M.
703 Oxford – LEFT Baylor, LEFT Karen, RIGHT Clemson, end Oxford
Books
511 Harvard – LEFT Oxford *Games*

Through experience I analyze each ad for content, location, sale time, and the personality or character type of the individual seller, as well as the neighborhood hosting each sale. Depending upon the products I am seeking for my arsenal, I review the ads to find those listings advertising my preferred items, such as *books*. Even though the ad may not offer "books," it may be highly likely that books will be for sale, when I consider all of the other ad information. Further, it may be quite likely that books will not be sold at this particular location and after analyzing everything I have at my disposal I can eliminate this sale as a potential target. It's part of the military intelligence mindset; there is objective data that must be gleaned in listing a target on the agenda, or eliminating it entirely.

Garage sales are a chance proposition. You never know what you will find, or if you will find anything to utilize in your endeavors. Nonetheless, the odds of locating target purchases can be increased in your favor by analyzing newspaper ads. Frequently, sales scheduled in older more established neighborhoods are a good source of inventory because their owners have lived longer and have likely accumulated more household effects. On the other hand, newer housing subdivisions are usually inhabited by younger people, who may have recently located there and normally possess fewer belongings to sell. Thus, how the ad is written provides a clue to the author and his domain. Read each ad carefully and try to decipher the not-too-obvious information. A *youthful* ad advertising baby items, toys, and maternity clothes contrasts with an older one offering a lifetime of treasures or a "house full of sales." Moving sales and inside sales usually indicate more items, as well as language in the ad itself indicating "everything must go," or similar wording. The location and neighborhood operations area in relation to your HQ can be a very important consideration. If you have to drive 20 miles and waste valuable time, this had better be a good sale. Familiarization with neighborhoods and sectors of the town is an important tool in your campaign strategy, so avoid areas that are economically distressed and not well maintained.

When the ad indicates activities will be conducted by multiple sellers such as "Five Family Garage Sale" set aside additional time to attend these garage sale locations. The reason for this is that multiple sellers typically will have different pricing and rules among the various participants at the same location. Also after your purchase selection it will take longer to check out because more time will be required for each family to handle the bookkeeping for their items being sold. In addition, each family's personality is likely different, and more time may be required for you to deal with one or more sellers of each family unit because each member will have a say about his or her particular effects. Sometimes the family representatives are not all present when bartering decisions have to be made, causing further delays.

The time of the sale is another important element, not only for scheduling purposes, but also in providing insight into the psyche of the seller. If, for example, the sale is advertised for 12:00 o'clock noon (which is rather late) this might indicate the person is not organized or motivated, and you may want to pass this one by. Or, he could be wealthy, sleeps late, and will not be difficult, and/or several other scenarios are just as likely. How items are listed and their order within the written ad itself can provide insight. If you are looking for books, and they are listed last in small print, you might surmise there are not very many books available at this sale. If the word "BOOKS" is capitalized and has the number one position in the ad, this might be noteworthy with more potential. And, if "BOOKS" is preceded by adjectives like *tons of*, *loads of*, or *library full of* you would be foolish not to check out this sale if you are looking for books! Other ad statements can significantly impact your consideration to attend a sale, such as those sellers who set the launch of the sale at a *very* specific moment in time. As you progress and gain experience, you will begin to notice terminology in ads suggesting that a dealer, professional, or other commercial enterprise may be the host, as well as other red flags to avoid in your quest for garage sale inventory. Finally, you will sporadically encounter *barnacles* on the trail. A barnacle is someone who is very frugal because he refuses to spend five dollars for an ad in the newspaper but has no compunction in capitalizing on the goodwill of others. He learns about sales scheduled by his neighbors and then posts signs on or near his property to divert your attention to the "unadvertised" sale at his HQ. Do not be confused by such diversion. I usually remain on course and do not exploit such alternative locations. With rising gasoline prices the cost of going to sales can add up significantly or result in substantial savings depending on your itinerary and the way you drive. Always drive within the posted speed limit, accelerate slowly, and regularly maintain your transport and tires to conserve fuel. The best way to save fuel is not use it! Keeping your plan on track and on schedule is always a challenge.

These are some of the considerations and nuances I check off in my mapping preparation. It is not an exact science. I commend this process to you. And, before I close this section, I must confess that occasionally I may overlook a little of this careful planning, and check out locations that might not squarely fit within normal operating procedure and guidelines. I have had occasional success in some instances when I purposely digress and divert. After all there is nothing like blind luck! However, I do not abandon my game plan often. Above all else, consider the words of the wise: "we often think in generalities, but we live in details." Stay alert, drive safely, and keep on schedule.

RULE NO. 14 RECON/GO EARLY, GO BACK, GO BEYOND

Every shot in this campaign has a purpose. Recently, a friend of mine approached me and told me he wanted to start his own garage sale Internet business—he wanted to do what I do. He asked me a series of questions. I explained the gist of my operation. He listened intently, thanked me, and went on his way. A month later I asked him how he was doing.

"Not too well," he replied. "I couldn't find anything anywhere!" "How do you do it?" He asked me in a frustrated tone while relating he had no luck at garage sales whatsoever. I inquired about his brief experiences. He had gone to a substantial number of sales. The areas and neighborhoods he probed were good ones, most of which I often frequented with success. I was perplexed. He had seemingly done everything I had instructed, but to no avail. Finally, I asked him:

"What time did you leave to go to the sales?"

"Nine thirty," he said.

I did not tell him, but I am usually finished for the day and back on base by that time. I had failed to tell my friend *to go early*. I am not going to bore you with the first arriving feathered friend being rewarded, but this business is highly competitive and takes dogged commitment. When I attack, I am the first person to open a sale, or I am in the top three early arrivals. When I am first in line, I get to pick and choose the items I want. The good belongings go fast. A couple weeks ago on Saturday I went to my usual 15 garage sales. About half of the sales started at 7:00 a.m. and the rest were advertised

GUERILLA GARAGE SALES

between 8:00 and 8:30 a.m. By 8:30 a.m. I was finished and heading back to my barracks. Enough said.

Going early also means that I preview sales whenever possible. Some charities and other organizations sponsoring rummage sales in our area allow buyers to come the day before and view the merchandise ahead of time. In some instances, for a small fee, I can purchase a preferential place in line for the sale or receive other benefits and discounts at the sale. Take advantage of these opportunities whenever possible. For no other reason, eliminating this sale from my itinerary saves time and is worth it, even if I do not find anything of interest. Also, I preview sales in my neighborhood or those being conducted by friends, relatives, and acquaintances. Frequently I am allowed to buy at the preview. This can be a tremendous advantage and saves time on garage sale day.

On the negative side, even though I may make a timely appearance, occasionally the pricing of some sellers may be too high at the opening. Some of these individuals may even have a self-imposed rule to not vary their stated prices until later in the sale day. If there are considerable items of interest to me at these sales, I may make a note and *go back* later in the day after I have exhausted my list. Hopefully by then garage sale reality has set in with the host, and I am more likely to purchase items for less. On other occasions, I leave my telephone number with the seller and ask him to call me at the end of the sale if certain items remain unsold, but this is usually not as successful as going back.

Another technique in my arsenal involves going back at the end of the day when the sale has closed. Typically, most garage sales do not liquidate everything and end up with leftovers. I make a point of choosing a couple of sales that are above average in merchandise content and return when they have closed their doors. I know when to return because most ads list the sales' duration. I purposely take my loveable little "K-9" *Sarge* with me to help break the ice, since this is a cold call. After introductions, I remind the homeowner that I had purchased from him previously. I ask him if I can take the remains of the sale "off his hands." Most people are tired by now and are agreeable. Sometimes I only request a few specific items that I prefer. Occasionally, I will offer to pay a token amount if there is initial hesitation by the seller. I expect to be asked what I am going to do with the contents, so I am prepared to give them a good answer. This is one of the better opportunities to acquire inventory in bulk at bargain basement prices. Every time a door closes, a window opens somewhere else.

A third creative option to consider in the acquisition of goods for re-sale is approaching sellers a day or two *before the sale date*. I am a Star Trek fan, and I am reminded of the famous "…and boldly go where no man has gone before" opening of each episode. I face some definite challenges when I opt for this bold type of uninvited encounters with the public, because I often meet resistance. Most people have traditional notions of fair play and may not cooperate. Some might be offended. Others are not that organized. If I am looking for specific items, the sale might not be set up at this early date. Often sellers do not know where everything is stored and they do not want to rummage for it. The few who consider my offer may require a premium for the aggravation, as opposed to the price I would pay on sale day because before the actual sale, the seller is not under any pressure such as he will likely face when the garage door opens and buyers swarm. So, in order to have any chance of success, I will need a *good reason* to convince the seller to sell in advance of the sale—a compelling story for this breach of social decorum. If I succeed and make a good buy, I am ahead of the game, but if I fail I may lose out completely and find myself excluded on sale day, depending upon the seller's disposition and the story I concocted. Nonetheless, this is where a buyer proves his or her worth and seizes the opportunity to excel. In sum, the guerilla strategy is one of parry, thrust, retreat, and try again.

RULE NO. 15 UTILIZE ALL RESOURCES AT YOUR DISPOSAL

Many people spend a great deal of effort and never get anywhere. Many attend garage sales like I do, but not the same *way* I do! Some may beat me to the opening, but I am still able to find worthwhile stock after they leave. There is an old saying that *it's not what we run into, it's how we deal with it that counts*. I maneuver at a rapid constant speed from one garage sale to the other. To save time when parking at a sale and being mindful of the rest of my itinerary, I think ahead and pre-position my vehicle so that I can drive to the next location easily without turning around or having my exit impeded. On several occasions when I was ready to leave, because of my planning failure I could not withdraw until other participants moved their vehicles. On other occasions when I failed to consider my coordinates in advance, I was forced to travel longer distances and waste time because I had not correctly positioned my vehicle.

GUERILLA GARAGE SALES

In my initial approach to any sale I always concentrate on finding the primary target such as *books*. Of course, I am constantly prepared to pounce on any secondary target such as any item in a sealed box, or anything that emerges and appears to be a good buy. My method is rote and simple. I focus my eyes and scan the entire sale quickly in a clockwise fashion to spot my targets. If I spot something interesting at "nine o'clock", I immediately maneuver closer to examine it. At "twelve o'clock" I may see more items, so I hold onto them until I can make a procurement decision to avoid interference from competitors. I have had items literally taken from my hands by other people at these events! Recently someone picked up a large decorative jar for the kitchen with *MARY ANN*, (my mother's name) on it because I was just gazing and contemplating instead of picking it up. Therefore, as a matter of practice, if I think there is a chance I might purchase an item, I hold onto it while on station and continue searching the remainder of the sales area for targets of opportunity. At this juncture, no matter how large the area may be, I cover the entire search radius briskly in a clockwise fashion. Then I completely cover the same territory again in a counter clockwise manner. I never cease to be amazed how many more targets I notice on the second pass than I did the first time, and how many different "blips" pop up in my range finder when I merely change direction. If I follow this method religiously, I regularly find the greatest number of items in the least amount of time.

If nothing of interest comes to the forefront before leaving, I do at least two more things–*look everywhere* and inquire of the host. I am reminded of numerous times this has happened, but the most memorable find that comes to mind occurred during my first three months in business. I was not the first person to reach this particular sale in a rural area. After scanning the tables lining the garage that day, I moved swiftly clockwise, then completely again counter clockwise. I was just about to leave, when I noticed a large cardboard box next to a large number of other boxes and miscellaneous items completely underneath one of the heavily laden tables of household goods and other miscellaneous effects. The box lid was half-closed, covered with plastic, and after closer inspection it appeared to contain a large doll. After a more cursory inspection I realized it was a full-sized Charlie McCarthy ventriloquist dummy in its original carrying case. The dummy and case was manufactured in New York City in 1961, and both were in mint condition! Without appearing to be too interested in the item and trying to hide my excitement, I casually asked the owner what she wanted for it. She gave me a very reasonable price. I knew I was going to purchase it, but since no one else was on the scene, I acted as if I was not too interested and returned it under the table. I then poked around a little longer before I picked up the item again and made a lower counteroffer before someone else arrived. The seller accepted, and I could hardly contain my elation when I left with this treasure. No matter how I look at things, there is always another way to see them. By process of elimination I do not limit my search to the tables and areas in plain view. I systematically exclude every possible location and hiding place at each sale. The average seller is not a businessman and normally does not put a lot of thought or effort into his sales display. He rarely knows the value of his own property, and it is not unusual for him to leave his most valuable items in a box with other possessions, underneath tables, in the corner, or not in plain sight. And, many sellers, due to a lack of display space or planning, do not put out all of their merchandise. Some of this property may still be sitting out of range elsewhere.

This reminds me of the second thing buyers need to do before leaving any garage sale–question the host. When I walk up on a sale I usually make a casual greeting, and I *ask the seller*, for example, if he has any books or movies for sale. I am often surprised at how many people do not inquire of the host and leave a sale when they do not see what they want. It is not uncommon for the seller to tell me he forgot to set the requested item out, and he has a whole box in the house or in the attic. It did not register with him until I mentioned it. I learn a lot in talking to sellers. They tell me they do not have any books this week for sale, but next week they are going to have another sale with tons of books. They tell me that their neighbor down the street has books for sale at another location. They tell me their daughter has books she will probably sell, and give me her telephone number. They tell me someone else is coming to this sale later with books. Talk to sellers. They can really help you with your buying decisions.

Be friendly and talkative when you are trying to learn about the condition of an item; you will get a better price in the end. Often the host will point out something you might have missed. Finally, you definitely need to ask the seller questions about a prospective purchase to try and determine age, condition, and other important factors. Sometimes *how* they answer the question is more important that what they actually say, so pay attention. However, on occasion Sellers may tell you they do not have certain items, but after a systematic search you may actually find them, so do not necessarily take their word and leave without making a thorough examination. It does not matter how much firepower you have if you do not use your intelligence.

GUERILLA GARAGE SALES

RULE NO. 16 NEWLY ISSUED STORES

Occasionally I may be wrong, but I am never in doubt. There is an unbreakable rule in this business. If I find an item for a dollar or less that is brand new, unopened in its original box or packaging, *I buy it*. Before I make that purchase, however, I determine all of my program coordinates and resolve several details. First, I must have some knowledge of the item or at least an educated guess as to its usefulness. My brand-new factory-sealed purchases to date include: a pedometer; hands-free kits for cellular phones, and other telephone accessories; board games, video game controller, computer software video games, and videos; books, office supplies, writing materials, stationery and greeting cards. I have also purchased new flashlights, a cordless electric screwdriver, a cordless electric toothbrush, and a carbon monoxide detector. Generally there are a variety of brand new home products and grooming and kitchen products available at most garage sales. Numerous products and devices are sold during holiday seasons and other special events year round. Carefully avoid products that are merely novel or "cute." Above all else, they must have practical uses. Do not buy late into a fad or passing fashion craze. Buy items in short supply that have high demand and are, therefore, more marketable. If there are millions already on the market, reconsider the purchase. The last thing a seller wants to do is put something out there that nobody wants. Furthermore, before buying, take the time to authenticate and confirm the item is *actually* factory sealed and has never been opened or used. In my mad guerilla rush on the trail, I sometimes fail to ascertain the integrity of packaging. If the original owner merely opened the item, but it was not used, it cannot be advertised as "brand new." If I am uncertain for any reason the final test is this: would my family, platoon, or I buy this product and actually use it?

Finally, (but not always) try to pick products whose appeal is not limited to a certain locale or region. Choose items that have universal appeal, save time, make work effortless, and are easy to ship. The size and weight of the item can be a deciding factor in not making a purchase if it becomes too expensive to pack and ship. Do not deviate from this objective unless good intelligence or prior field experience dictates otherwise. Correct adherence to this rule is the best way to insure arrival of checks in the e-mail.

RULE NO. 17 LANDMINES TO AVOID ON BIVOUAC AND IN THE FIELD

Something goes wrong because it always does, but you only prosper through adversity. This is the captain speaking. Our mission is not going to be affected by common errors made by raw recruits. If you want to be elite, commit this not-to-do-list to memory, soldier:

1.   Do not attend any sales after the first day unless you have time to kill or are scavenging the remains at the sale's end because all of the gems have been mined. Further you might inadvertently attend the same sale if you do not review your prior itineraries in advance to be certain there was not a recent event at the same address.

2.   Do not fail to inspect sales items for imperfections, repairs, and flaws before purchasing. Condition affects value. In the heat and excitement of battle, it is common to neglect close inspection of potential purchases, however not all flaws are visible; some are revealed by cleaning away dirt and grime and others may be found simply by touch. There is a low-tech way to find cracks in glassware and porcelain—a robust thump with your finger will reveal a dull thud or a hardy ring, depending upon whether or not a hairline crack is present. Some dishonest vendors cover up imperfections with price tags, paint, and other substances. Before you spend *always* verify condition. Take price tags off right after the sale; the longer they stay on the item the harder they are to remove. Open CDs, Videos, and DVDs to verify they are correct, everything is intact, and there are no visible signs of damage or wear. Shake gently to see if there is breakage. Ask the seller questions about the merchandise. What he says and how he answers the questions will help you with your purchasing decisions.

3.   Do not hesitate. When in doubt, buy it right away. If you don't someone else will beat you to it. I cannot tell you how many times I have gone back for an item after a brief time lapse, only to find it was gone. If you are thinking about an item at the sale, pick it up and carry it around while you decide, before someone else picks it up.

GUERILLA GARAGE SALES

4.   Do not overpay. If the price is not right, walk away.

5.   Do not be fooled by reproductions. If you don't know the difference, learn, or don't make a purchase. If it looks too good it probably is a reproduction.

6.   Do not buy junk simply because the price seems too cheap to resist. The goal is to sell for a profit not recycle, donate, and lose money.

7.   Do not set down items at the sales table or leave them unattended. Other buyers *will* appropriate them. There is not a fairness doctrine at garage sales and whoever has possession usually wins. On one occasion I purchased a steamer trunk at a Junior League Sale. In order to check out I had to produce an invoice for each item. To continue shopping unburdened with such a large piece in tow, I took the trunk to the front checkout, informed one of the attendants, and retained the accompanying invoice. Later when I went to check out, another customer was attempting to purchase my item. Because I retained the invoice I was the one who left with the trunk!

8.   Whenever purchasing large items such as furniture or appliances, be prepared to immediately remove it from the seller's premises. If not, when you return to the sale, the seller may refund your purchase price and regret to inform you that another buyer made him an offer he couldn't refuse. If you are unable to take immediate possession for any reason, take a part of the item with you such as cushions, drawers, shelves, or other components, to insure it cannot be re-sold to another buyer.

9.   Do not repair or paint an item and then try to sell it without informing the buyer.

10.   Do not clean, paint, or touch up antiques or collectibles without expert advice. The general rule is that anything that alters the original patina (surface coating or finish of an object) of a collectible or antique, usually impacts the value negatively.

11.   After some experience you can usually tell if a garage sale will be good in the first five minutes. If the sale is lackluster do not stay more than five minutes

CASH HOFFMAN

after following all of the other rules of engagement. Make the best use of your time. There are plenty of other sales opportunities during the campaign.

12.   If I do not take possession of the item I know there is no sale. Whenever I leave empty-handed the seller can always sell to someone else no matter what they say.

13.   Do not buy anything powered by electricity or batteries without testing on the spot before you buy. This obviously takes pre-planning. Carry batteries and, in your clockwise reconnaissance, locate an electrical outlet you can reach quickly and easily. There are no substitutes for avoiding landmines in the field, overcoming the competition, and winning the battle.

IV

OPERATION AUCTION

Another timeworn method for purchasing inventory for resale is the typical auction. According to Wikipedia, the free encyclopedia, "[a]n *auction* is the process of buying and selling things by offering them up for bid, taking bids, and then selling the item to the highest bidder." A highly skilled professional called an *auctioneer* conducts the live auction and oversees the bidding. Prior to the sale, auction inventory is catalogued with a unique number. Each offering for sale is referred to as a *"lot"* whether containing one or more items. The bidding in an English, or "outcry" auction is a public event utilizing an ascending bid format to encourage participants to bid openly against each other and maximize the final sales price. You will often find several types of auction formats being utilized during the same sale. Whenever there are duplicates of the same item being sold, the auctioneer will often deploy the Dutch format. The traditional Dutch auction begins with a high asking price that is proffered and incrementally lowered by the auctioneer until someone accepts his last announced offer. Dutch auctions normally end when the auctioneer accepts the first announced bid from the floor. The winning bidder may claim as many of the items as he wants at the gavel price. If there are remaining unclaimed items, the auctioneer may allow the next highest bidder to claim all or a portion of the remainder. Occasionally anyone may be allowed to jump in and buy the remaining items at the first high bid amount. This process is continued until all the duplicates are sold or withdrawn. There are silent auctions, sealed bid auctions, and several other variations, but for our purposes we will concentrate on live English auctions.

Auctions are as old as civilization itself. If you can think of an item to buy, it has probably been sold at auction. Because the average person has never

CASH HOFFMAN

participated in a traditional auction, a certain mystique has emerged over the years. Most are somewhat uninformed about the process. Before creation of the Internet it was not a commonplace event—few people rarely purchased anything by way of auction. In the past it was viewed as an activity pursued mainly by wealthy individuals, serious collectors, the elite, or professionals. Movies and television shows have furthered this myth by portraying ordinary people getting in serious difficulty at auctions because they did not know how to conduct themselves. Merely scratching a nose, the adjustment of a cap, or hair arranging would apparently cause the unintended purchase of expensive antiques or artwork. Nothing is further from the truth. In spite of this prevailing view even today, any bidder, with minimum knowledge, can successfully compete at auction. You just need to learn a few simple rules and bidding strategies before you try it yourself. The main thing to remember is to arrive early and expect to stay a while. If you want a good parking place, time to register, and find a good seat, it is a good idea to get to the auction several hours before the sale begins. If you are attending an outdoor auction, take a chair, protection from the elements, and something to eat and drink (check ahead, most auction houses will not allow food or drink if there is a concession lease on the premises). There are several important preliminary matters to resolve before you can bid, however. The following links may be helpful in locating the principal players and/or important auctions in your area: http://www.worldartantiques.com/AuctionHouses.htm, a national directory of auction houses, including business names, locations and contact information, and http://www.americanaexchange.com/auctions/ actionlistings.asp, a nation-wide calendar of book auctions, including detailed information about major auction houses and links to websites.

Assuming you have located an auction to attend, as a new bidder before you can participate in the sale you have to register with the auction house and arrange for any credit in advance. Inquire if the house charges a *buyer's premium*. After a hectic bidding war followed by the fall of the auctioneer's hammer, it is sometimes customary to pay the amount of your winning bid plus a fee. The fee added to the winning bid is called a buyer's premium, and it is paid to the auction house to cover advertising and other auction expenses. Unless the notice of sale specifically states to the contrary, always take cash to pay for your purchases. There is normally no charge to register, but most auction houses require two forms of identification—a picture I.D. and a credit card. At registration, the sponsor of the sale provides a bidding card or paddle emblazoned with large, bold numbers identifying each bidder. You do

GUERILLA GARAGE SALES

not necessarily have to display your bidding identification while you bid, but you must provide your number to the auctioneer each time you win. The auctioneer or an assistant will then write your individual paddle number directly on the winning lot. They will also make a notation on other paperwork that will be forwarded to the auction office during the sale, where a running tally of all purchases is maintained. Payment must be made at the end of the auction. You are required to pay for all your purchases at the office and take possession of your sale items the same day. To keep track of my purchases, I also write all of my winning lot numbers on the back of my bidding card.

After registration, take sufficient time to review all of the lots being offered for sale. Auction houses always put their lots up for inspection and presale viewing by the public. Sometimes they extend the viewing for several days in advance of the sale. The viewing is free of charge. Use as much time as you have to look at everything carefully. Research! Research! Research! Look, touch, handle the merchandise, and ask questions about everything that interests you. Most lots are sold *AS IS*, which is short for: *as is where is and with all faults*. An "*as is* sale" means the seller is *not* standing behind the quality of the goods nor is he making any representations, express or implied as to its condition. The buyer assumes *the entire risk of loss!* Therefore the buyer must rely solely on his own inspection. There is not even an implied warranty by the seller that the goods are merchantable, fit for a specific purpose, or even suitable for the purpose for which such goods are normally used. Be certain you understand the legal and practical effect of this phrase before you buy at auction or anywhere else. If you do not have an opportunity to view the lots prior to the sale, it would not be advisable to bid during the auction. The auctioneer will not describe the lot in any detail and he will make it abundantly clear that he knows very little about any of the goods. To add levity to the proceedings, some auctioneers make silly comments about the merchandise. They may even describe some ridiculous way to use the item, as if they do know what they are selling. There are usually employees of the auction house available on the floor to assist you with viewing and inspecting the auction lots prior to the sale. As you personally assess the sale's merchandise, try to determine:

✠ The condition of each item
✠ Whether it has been repaired or restored
✠ Any distinguishing marks or other identification, signatures, dates, etc.

CASH HOFFMAN

- ✠ Manufacturer or artist who made it
- ✠ Date of manufacture or creation
- ✠ Whether it is faux, knockoff, reproduction, or authentic
- ✠ Its value, rarity, or historical importance
- ✠ Any other important features or characteristics

While perusing the merchandise during your presale inspection, make notations regarding each lot you are considering to purchase. Write down the applicable lot number. Establish the maximum price you are willing to bid ahead of time on each one and write it down. This exercise will help you to stay grounded whenever you are tempted on the spur of the moment (and you will be) in the live-action salesroom to overpay during the heat of battle. There are very few experiences like the energy of a live auction. Whenever possible, try to talk to the auctioneer on the floor prior to the sale. Attempt to develop rapport, get a feel for his style, and how he runs things. Every auctioneer has a different way of working the crowd. Each one has a unique sense of humor, and employs a different method and tempo to generate bids. The good ones are masters at eliciting bids from the crowd. In many ways it is like a live performance on stage and the auctioneer is the master of ceremonies. The more you get to know an auctioneer's style the more comfortable you will be when you bid. Sometimes when I am interested in only one lot, I ask the auctioneer or his staff to bring it on the floor early so I do not have to wait around all day to bid. I have been accommodated on several occasions when there was a large crowd and it was not against the policy of the sponsor. Normally this practice is not allowed because the auction house wants everyone to stay and bid on every lot.

The next decision you need to make is where to sit during the proceedings. As a general rule, seating is first come first serve. There are no reservations, so arrive early. If you want to keep track of the competition, sit toward the rear of the auditorium. Participants who want to maintain their privacy sit closer to the front. Being up front also brings you closer to the goods and the auctioneer. This affords you a superior view of the proceedings and it easier to hear. There are numerous individuals who work in tandem with the auctioneer. When the auctioneer announces the next lot for sale, several helpers bring the goods to the forefront for everyone to see. Sometimes they hoist it up and parade it around the room in front of the crowd during the bidding to maintain interest. When the bidding is closed, they either return it to the warehouse, or carry it to the pickup area to be claimed by the winning bidder. There are several other individuals called *bid spotters*, who are employees of the auction house and play a dual role during the auction. Bid spotters assist the auctioneer in recognizing and confirming the bids throughout the room, especially those he may not notice. Moreover, experienced bidders who want to remain anonymous, often work with bid spotters who will bid on their behalf. Before the sale begins they agree on certain secure signals the bidder will make to the spotter during the auction. Once the spotter has identified such a bid, the auctioneer will take the bid directly from the spotter and no one will know the actual bidder's identity. Spotters also add to the atmosphere of the sale by yelling out bid amounts and revving up the crowd during the sale much like carnival barkers. Although bid spotters may appear to have a lot of latitude, the auctioneer is always in control.

The auctioneer begins the proceedings by introducing himself and making announcements. There are two types of auctions—absolute and reserve. *Absolute auctions* are free of liens or encumbrances, with a bona fide intention to transfer ownership regardless of the amount of the highest and last bid, to the high bidder without restriction. This means that the seller agrees to sell regardless of the final high bid price and there are no minimum bids or reserve. The seller and no one on his behalf may bid at an absolute auction. Goods are generally sold *"with reserve,"* however. With *"reserve"* means the goods may be offered subject to the seller's right to reject the final bid outright, or prior to the sale he may set a certain minimum price that must be met before he will relinquish ownership. Unless otherwise explicitly announced, an auction sale is presumed to be a reserve auction. It is in the discretion of the auctioneer to announce when the reserve has been met. The seller or his agents may bid at a reserve sale after full disclosure to all participants. The purpose of a reserve is to create a safety net for the seller, so that he does not have to accept an unreasonable price. An auction without reserve means an absolute auction.

After briefly covering the rules, the auctioneer may open the bidding on any lot he chooses by placing his own bid in play, the seller's reserve, an absentee bid, or a telephone bid. The auctioneer decides the bidding increments to be used during the auction, which by custom in the industry is usually increased by ten per cent on each and every consecutive succeeding bid. If the bid opens with $200.00, the next bid would be $220.00, $240.00, and so on. Auctioneers need a consistent standard for offers made at an auction to establish a pace or rhythm to drive the bidding. Moreover, skilled bidders and bid spotters need to know the incremental bidding pattern to bid correctly and keep up with the flow. Some bidders may try to change the rhythm and interfere with this incremental pattern. This device is also used to set a bid limit. One such procedure is called "bid cutting." This occurs when a bidder increases the bid, but fails to offer the full increment. In our third example bid above, a bidder might cut the bid by offering $230.00 instead of the expected $240.00. At this point the auctioneer may accept or reject such a bid. Normal business practice dictates that if the auctioneer believes the bidder is truly setting a limit, he may allow him to cut the bid once, but then reject any further bid cutting, otherwise it will interfere with the bidding rhythm by lowering the incremental rate. Militant bidders may also interfere with the pace of the bidding by *increasing* bid increments exponentially. In our third example bid above, a bidder might increase his bid by offering $500.00 instead of $240.00. This is called "jumping the bid." Surprisingly, even though this interferes with the pace of the auction just as much as bid cutting, I have never seen an auctioneer refuse a bid jump. Besides setting a limit, bid jumping is also a device that is used to chill further bidding. It acts as a signal to other potential bidders who may be interested in the same lot that this bidder will outbid anyone who comes near. If you have limited funds, this device may work for you if you bid jump to your limit very early in the bidding to deter other bidders. Nonetheless, this practice does not normally deter experienced bidders and other professionals.

When bidding you need to decide in advance how you want to communicate to the auctioneer that you are placing a bid. Be certain that the auctioneer can clearly see you and recognize your signals. It is possible to nod your head or make certain gestures, but the easiest way to bid is to hold up your paddle or bidding card. If you have not been bidding and you come into the bid process late in the game, a gesture or other subtle form of communication might not be noticed or accepted and you could lose the bid. Adopt a late bidding strategy. Wait to bid at the last moment. Every time you bid someone else could respond and increase the price. Therefore, take your time and save your money. The best times to bid are during the beginning of the auction before everyone is warmed up and at the end of the auction when everyone is tired and out of money. Leave your ego at home and take control of your emotions. Do not get in a bidding war just to keep someone else from buying. Although it is a rare occurrence, the other person raising the bid could be aligned with the auction house or the owner of the goods. Also, you could be the victim of a *phantom bid*. This is a bid recognized by the auctioneer against you that was never made. Unless you know the identity of the other bidder, a raise by you could be against yourself. Reputable auctioneers often identify whose bid is being recognized by acknowledging: "the lady in the yellow hat on the back row," or "it is the young man's bid in the blue shirt by the left aisle," or "it is yours sir, the gentlemen in the suit by the exit," etc. This practice recognizes the current bid holder and signals everyone else to continue bidding. Of course in the final analysis, the best defense against all unscrupulous activity is not to bid more than the item is worth.

There are certain terms and phrases customarily practiced in the industry that a beginner needs to learn. When the end of bidding is imminent, the auctioneer may say things like "last chance," "fair warning," or "all through then," before bringing down the gavel on a lot. Sometimes a bid may be placed "with the hammer" at the same moment the gavel is coming down. The auctioneer has the option to let the sale stand or reopen the bidding. The phrases "passed," or "bought in" after the gavel falls means the item was not sold. "Reserve" is the absolute minimum price the consignor of a lot will accept. Only the consignor and the auctioneer know the reserve price. If the reserve is not met, the property will be returned to the consignor. An "absentee bid" or "order bid" is placed with the auction company prior to the sale on behalf of someone who cannot attend in person. This type of bid may be referred to as being "in the book."

There are several strategic advantages associated with the live auction business model:

🖐 Absentee bids can be placed to set a limit, avoid involvement in the emotion of the moment, and maintain the privacy of the bidder

🖐 Technical glitches cannot interfere with your bidding like a computer crash or losing your internet provider

🖐 Easier to inspect the goods (some things have to be seen live in three full dimensions; digital cameras can unintentionally hide a lot of detail)

🖐 You have a better sense of the competition around you

🖐 Being in the same room in sight of the sales item; usually a small number of bidders (however it only takes one person to push the price to a ridiculous level)

- Set your own price

- Fraud is more difficult—prior to sale you are allowed to inspect, then bid, and take the goods with you the same day

- Large variety of goods to choose from in one place

- Final price not subject to dealer mark-up or other handling fees

- Possible to find a good bargain

- No time constraints, like a garage sale, items will be sold same day

- Can be an enjoyable social event, there is nothing like the energy of a well-run live auction

The major disadvantage of live auction trading is that many get caught up in the thrill of the hunt. They get a rush during the bidding process similar to gambling. This can adversely affect pricing. Rivalry amongst competing bidders can produce distorted prices far beyond fair market value when emotion, envy, and ego overcome reason. The best weapons against auction abuse are knowledge and personal discipline. You can't fight everyone at once.

V

INTERDICT ESTATE SALES

Another type of sale you may attend in the never-ending pursuit of goods and wares is an *estate sale*. Sometimes called a *living estate sale* or *tag sale*, this event differs considerably from garage sales and yard sales. An estate sale is typically the liquidation of an entire household of personal property and belongings of one family. Besides furniture and appliances, this type of sale normally includes the entire spectrum of property you might find in most homes, such as pictures, cookware, appliances, linens, and clothing. It also encompasses a large cross section of other household and personal articles, antiques, and collectibles. This event is conducted primarily in two distinct ways. The family of the deceased (or disabled person moving into assisted living quarters) organizes a sale of the property in a manner similar to the garage sale model, but it is generally conducted throughout the entire premises of the home or location, and not limited to the garage. You are free to shop and browse in someone else's living quarters. This was a very weird experience for me the first time I attended an estate sale. It was a little eerie as I soon found myself going room to room, looking in drawers, and going through boxes of another person's property. I realized that this was everything someone had, and everything they were ever going to have.

The sale tends to last several consecutive days until the bulk of the property is liquidated. Much like the homeowner who conducts the average neighborhood garage sale, family members in an estate sale setting are likely not equipped to appraise and sell most of the contents of a home. If the estate sale is a family run operation, you should attend early and the likelihood of finding a bargain is greatly enhanced. Most families realize their shortcomings in this regard however, and choose to have the sale conducted by an auction house, liquidating company, or dealer. These professionals are fully aware of market value of the belongings. Through their efforts a sale will likely yield the greatest rate of return for the family and frustrate your hopes of securing a great deal. When you go to professionally-run estate sale, even though it may be conducted in the family home, in my opinion it often feels like walking through an antique store when it comes to pricing. Although item pricing may be lowered by the sale professional during the ensuing days, a bargain is usually difficult to find. Whenever the bulk of one estate does not warrant a sale on its own merits, the professional conducting the sale, will put several smaller estates together to make one sale. They are required by law to make this fact known. Sometimes the professional liquidator may include some of its inventory in the sale without disclosing this fact to the public. This fraudulent practice is called *home packing*. Buyers should always beware! Never assume that an item being offered for sale actually belonged to the estate or the family named in the estate sale advertisements, without proper documentation or provenance. If the items being offered for sale do not seem to coordinate with other goods located throughout the house, something might be amiss. When there appears to be an overabundance of certain furnishings like too many chairs or multiple duplicates of furniture, accessories, or other household goods, this could be a sign of "packing." Whenever you get the feeling that certain property located in the home does not seem to belong, be suspicious. Since you will not be dealing with the actual owner of the property, make a thorough inspection. Ask questions and if you are not satisfied with the response, shop elsewhere. At the end of the sale the company liquidating the estate often purchases the leftovers from the family, or the remains may be sold at a traditional auction scheduled at a later date. This is the main reason you probably will not find a treasure with a garage sale price. Occasionally this may be reversed. The operator of an estate sale will simply conduct a live auction on site and forego an estate sale entirely. Following the auction the remains may be purchased in bulk by the auction house. The normal rules of live auctions apply should you decide to attend an estate auction. Nonetheless, if you are in the market for antiques and collectibles, estate sales are the place you want to be. Some things never change. Some things never stay the same.

VI

MASSING MATERIEL

Anything worth having in life is hard to get, and things that are easy to get or achieve generally don't mean much. Call it the entrepreneur's dilemma, you have a philosophy and everything in place to satisfy customers, but you do not have anything to sell. Everyone would agree with the following:

No inventory, no business.

That is why the number one concern of all e-commerce sellers is securing a never-ending supply of inventory to sustain a constant revenue stream. Everything else is secondary. What secret knowledge do successful online merchants possess that we do not have? Is there a path to progress, a logical pursuit to success? How do you compete for merchandise to sell online? We have spent considerable time on garage sales, auctions, and estate sales as a primary source to implement our overall marketing plan. There are other available avenues known to the pros that you may want to tap for goods to sell in your business. To find other suitable markets and *materiel,* look in the local yellow pages and contact local wholesalers and distributors. You can save on shipping and develop local business contacts. Depending on your requirements, *Overstock.com* and *Liquidations.com* are business supply sources, as well as accessing the *www.globalsources.com* web site.

On occasion I have attended storage warehouse sales advertised in my local newspaper. I also called the local storage facilities in my area and placed my name on their mailing list for future sales. Individuals and businesses often rent storage bins, commercial locker space, and public storage buildings to house their belongings and all sorts of goods. The random cruelty of our world is that many renters fall behind in their monthly rental payments. After some period of non-payment the landlord can change the locks and evict the occupant. When the landlord gives proper legal notice to the original owner to pay for the stored personal property and he defaults, an auction of the contents can be conducted to recoup the landlord's fees and expenses. Storage unit auctions are distinct. I have been to some where they allow you to view the property prior to sale and others did not. I have bid at auctions where property items were sold individually. Others accepted bids only by the box. In this latter instance, often you could only see whatever was on top of the carton without knowing if anything of value lay beneath the exposed contents. Some auctioneers just lifted the sliding door to the unit and asked for one bid on everything. You never know what you will find. I have bought boxes of junk and empty boxes. I have found money in clothing and other items. Of course all sales are *AS IS!* If you secure the winning bid on the entire contents, you generally have to remove the property within 24 hours. You may also be required to police the storage unit by removing all trash and debris, and sweep it clean. If possible, look for water damage, mildew, and rodent infestation before you bid. In retrospect we have a much easier life today than the average ancient Roman Citizen who failed to take care of his debts:

"After the judicial proof or confession of the debt, 30 days of grace were allowed before a Roman was delivered into the power of his fellow-citizen. In this private prison, 12 ounces of rice were his daily food; he might be bound with a chain of 15 pounds weight; and his misery was thrice exposed in the market-place, to solicit the compassion of his friends and countrymen. At the expiration of 30 days the debt was discharged by the loss of liberty or life; the insolvent debtor was either put to death or sold in foreign slavery beyond the Tiber; but, if several creditors were alike obstinate and unrelenting, they might legally dismember his body, and satiate their revenge by this horrid partition." – Edward Gibbon, The History of The Decline and Fall of the Roman Empire.

For thousands of years people have been selling their odds and ends in open-air flea markets or wherever the populace congregated. In the Middle East, according to the Bible, this was an area near the Temple. Ancient Greeks called their market *Agora*. The Roman Empire had its *Forum*. Although the exact origin of the term *Flea Market* is unknown, the use of this description to refer to a sale first appeared in print in France in the 1860's. In 1998 Albert LaFarge's wrote an article that was published in Today's Flea

Market magazine (winter edition) entitled "What is a Flea Market." His explanation mirrors the most commonly-held belief that flea market…"is a literal translation of the French *marche aux puces*, an outdoor bazaar in Paris, France, named after those pesky little parasites of the order Siphonaptera (or 'wingless bloodsucker') that infested the upholstery of old furniture brought out for sale." Today's flea market is an open-air or indoor facility that rents space to vendors who in turn offer goods and services to the general public. It has been estimated there are over 20,000 flea markets operating each weekend across America, totaling more than $5 billion dollars in sales. Flea markets are not inherently better or worse than any other venue. The main negative is a marche aux puces is operated by a merchant or vendor— bargains will be difficult to find! The following websites may be helpful: http://www.antiqueguide.net/index2.html features a store locator with an interactive U.S.A. map. http://www.fleamarketguide.com. The flea market locator is indexed by state.

Another product source is charities and thrift stores. Three organizations head the list of non-profit national entities you should consider for periodic visit—Goodwill Industries, The Salvation Army, and St. Vincent de Paul stores.

The Salvation Army began through the efforts of William Booth in London, England in July of 1865. It is a well-recognized legal entity with a military structure and is still going strong. The familiar Red Shield is prominently displayed over 9,600 service centers in the United States that sell second hand belongings for benefit of charity.

Goodwill Industries was founded in 1902 in Boston, Massachusetts by Edgar J. Helms, a Methodist Minister. "A hand up, not a hand out," was the early motto of this organization that opened its doors to anyone willing to work and has touched the lives of over 5 million people in the past century. The retail sale of donated goods is still its single largest revenue source. Encompassing 211 member organizations in the United States, Canada, and other countries, Goodwill remains a worldwide benevolence movement.

The child of poor parents in the village of Pouy in Gascony, France around 1580, Vincent de Paul was ordained priest in 1600. His works of compassion as a servant of God throughout his life are innumerable, but charity was his predominant virtue and he remained deeply rooted in humility. Ironically he became the patron saint of charity. Today, known for its network of re-sale thrift shops, *St. Vincent de Paul* is well known throughout the world as an international, non-profit, charitable organization, which has a rich history of service to the needy.

Not everyone chooses to sell used belongings in a flea market or a yard sale. Many prefer to donate to these mega-charities and others like them that accept everything from automobiles to clothing and help employ the disabled and disadvantaged. They operate out of pleasant retail brick and mortar storefronts and usually have several convenient locations for the public to drop-off donations. In return, donors receive the satisfaction of providing hope, dignity, and independence to the less fortunate. Most stores introduce used merchandise weekly. I pinpoint when each store in my area stocks new items, and try to be there early. As a practical matter it is not feasible for me to sell half of my guerilla garage sale purchases. There is nothing wrong with the items. After research I find that I simply cannot list and sell them in my business for a reasonable profit. Accordingly, I donate these items to these charities and receive a federal income tax deduction in return. The greatest reward is the satisfaction of helping others through charity and I urge you to do the same.

I am a believer in the theory that the essence of genius is simplicity itself. To drum up business while standing in line at the Post Office or running errands I had a special multi-colored T-shirt made. It advertised the following: *ASK ME ABOUT SELLING FOR YOU ONLINE,* followed by my e-mail address in bold letters. I have placed an ad in the newspaper announcing that I buy books and videos. I have also advertised in the paper that I will pick up garage sale leftovers. Finally, when you need to get started or hit a dead end, simply go to a search engine online and type in what you are looking for. You are bound to find something that will point you in the right direction. Some of the most popular online search engines include the following:

http://www.google.com
http://www.mamma.com
http://www.dogpile.com
http://www.yahoo.com

It's a different world now. All you have to do is decide what to do with the time that was given to you.

VII

KNOW YOUR ARSENAL

I bought three items at only the second garage sale I attended. My purchases included a Ninja Turtles lunchbox, two Power Rangers water bottles, and a Casper the Ghost cup. I spent a total of seventy-five cents. Although I began each item for sale on *eBay* at ninety-nine cents, I received $26.00 for the water bottles, the lunchbox sold for $12.00, and the cup went for $10.00. It was blind luck on my part, but each of these items was highly sought after by collectors. I like watching antique and collector programs on television, like *Antiques Roadshow*. During the period of time I first launched my own business I remember seeing one of those TV programs on the subject of collectibles for the new millennium. The host began the segment by making the statement that there are collectors throughout the world for just about everything. He drove home the point that he was not just talking about the traditional collections that come to mind that we all remember from our youth, like stamps, coins, pocket knives, marbles, and *Coca Cola* memorabilia. He went on to illustrate that there was one man who collected toilet paper, and that he had every type that was ever manufactured! Even though you need to specialize, it is essential to have some general knowledge of the collectibles market and what collectors are buying. Another example to illustrate this point is when I bought a pair of small ceramic Llamas at a church bazaar for $1.00. They had great detail, were finely made, embodied very delicate features, and were in great condition. At the end of the eBay auction I realized $56.00 from the sales proceeds. Several collectors were trying to outbid each other for this prize. I know they were collectors because after the auction I researched their buying history and learned they were buying Llama memorabilia almost exclusively. I have never seen another Llama since.

During the first two years of this guerilla garage sales campaign, my father accompanied me, because I was not old enough to drive. On numerous occasions he would direct my attention to certain items and urge me to purchase them for resale in my business, but I was reluctant to take his advice. Often he would pick up dollhouses, dollhouse furniture, books, and other items of interest to females—"girl stuff"—but I was resistant to any of his suggestions and would have none of it. Call me crazy, but I did not want people to think I was young man interested in these items. After all, I was a "straight guy" and I did not have a "queer eye." To make a point, my dad would purchase the items for his own account and sell them on *eBay* for a healthy profit, which did not escape my attention. And, Dad never stopped talking to me. I remember the breakthrough conversation we had. He propounded the following questions to me:

"Do you want to ignore more than one-half of the potential customers in the entire world who can purchase your goods? Are you willing to make a conscious decision to turn away the majority of shoppers who may buy from you, for no good reason?" he asked.

"What do you mean?" I turned the question back to him, defensively.

"Who do you think does the majority of shopping and spends most of the household income in this country?" he retorted with almost righteous indignation. "Women!" he exclaimed, as he went on to explain the division of labor in the real world, and Marketing 101 to me.

One of the first things I bought after following my father's advice was a Barbie Dollhouse. It was in early December. I paid $3.00 for it and sold it a week later for $59.00. On another occasion I attended a yard sale out in the country. A chain link fence surrounded the site. The entire fence was so covered with various types of clothing that you could not see the yard or anything in it. It was late in the day. When I looked over the fence there was nothing of interest to me remaining for sale. As I turned to leave, I noticed a clear plastic garment bag hanging on the fence containing something inside it that looked like leather. After closer inspection, I realized it was a like new woman's buckskin leather jacket. The garment bag was from a commercial cleaning establishment and a tag attached to the bag indicated that the jacket had just been professionally cleaned. Standing by the fence, I picked it up and held it in the air, asking the owner how much. The reply was one dollar. After I got home and removed the contents from the bag, I found that besides the jacket, also draped on the hanger was a like new leather skirt. Within ten days I sold the jacket for $75.00 and the skirt sold for $50.00.

GUERILLA GARAGE SALES

In a world full of irritating clichés and cloying catch phrases, the word "marketing" leaves most people cold. It rates near the bottom of human activity somewhere in the neighborhood of telephone solicitation. In commerce and industry this is serious business, however, and no worthwhile enterprise can survive without practicing some form of it. Everyone knows that creating a marketing plan is an important element to the overall success of a company or new product introduction. Did you know that to be successful you have to spend 80% of your time marketing your business? On the surface, this is a daunting task, however, according to basic marketing principles you only need a little theory to practice and apply, and the rest comes naturally. But, you have to practice it every day. Most people think marketing is advertising, including some businessmen who do not understand the basic components of marketing. Advertising is a type of marketing, but marketing is much more than advertising. Advertising is only the first step in the marketing process. If marketing were a song, advertising would only be a few bars. According to *Theodore Levitt*, "what usually gets emphasized is selling, not marketing. This is a mistake, since selling focuses on the needs of the seller, while marketing concentrates on the needs of the buyer." You must have your customers in mind from the first moment you begin.

Furthermore, marketing is not to be confused with sales—it is the set of activities: used to bring potential customers to your business, motivate them to buy your products for more than the cost to you, and actually get them to buy again. The real marketing starts when a customer e-mails you with a question, when he buys something, when you ship his item, when he registers a complaint or gives you "Feedback", and whether or not he is a repeat customer. All are marketing functions. In a nutshell, marketing is how you define your merchandise, promote it, distribute it, and maintain a relationship with your customers. There are several basic marketing points contained in this book which I follow, and you should consider.

Whenever you sell a product you need to have some concept of the demographics relating to the targeted sales group, including age, income, sex, and education, to name a few. All of your efforts to communicate with this core group beginning with the ad design, graphics, colors, backgrounds, type fonts, and copy content, need to be in tune with your sales audience. If you attempt to reach a younger audience, you would normally be less sophisticated in your approach than toward a group comprised mainly of older businessmen. Likewise, advertising focusing mostly on women would normally bear no resemblance to the content or makeup you would employ with solely men in mind. Making a conscious effort to incorporate these basic marketing principals into your overall business plan will reap definite dividends. Your advertising and business communications will look and feel professional. Everything will not only look right, it will perform as intended, and reach the target audience. This involves homework, constant planning, and dedication to the task at hand. Despite this colossal undertaking, remember, you eat an elephant one bite at a time.

VIII

KP DETAIL

After the arduous campaign of amassing and stockpiling inventory, particularly used merchandise, you quickly learn that not all treasures and stores are in brand new condition. After all, that's usually why you get such a good buy in the first place. Frequently some items need cleaning or touching up in order to restore their former luster and value, but this is not necessarily a costly venture. No matter what, our mission is not going to be compromised by the condition of our cache. Every unit has its favorite cadre of cleaning supplies and restoration methods. Most chemical agents you will need for this purpose can be found in your barracks in the wash room, storeroom, or medicine cabinet. Because time is of the essence in your overall mission, upon your return to base, you will not be able to immediately touch up your sale valuables. Moreover, you do not need a workshop or special space to conduct recovery operations, but strive to create storage boxes to keep items and supplies in a central location until you can give them proper attention. When you begin the cleaning process, try to use a clean, well-lit, properly ventilated area. After you have detailed an item, before it passes final inspection, view it in natural sunlight. This will reveal flaws or unflattering surfaces that may not be completely noticeable in artificial light. The following is a good selection of cleaning supplies I routinely use: liquid soap, Windex glass cleaner, Comet cleanser, Bar Keeper's Friend, ammonia, Clorox, fingernail polish remover, cornstarch, baking soda, brass polish, Formula 409, rubbing alcohol, lemon oil, furniture polish, and Goo Gone. My basic repair supply list contains: cleaning cloths, WD-40, lubrication oil, a gum eraser, an assortment of small paint brushes, toothbrushes, and make-up brushes, Q-tips, Magic Markers, Sharpies, a container of Super Glue, glue sticks, Crayons, paper table napkins, Elmer's glue, a glue gun, sand paper, emery boards, and clamps to hold items being glued.

In my limited experience I have learned that cleaning and restoring the condition of collectibles and household goods is almost an art form. Furthermore, in most instances, this process is wholly trial and error. A method may work perfectly for one collectible, but fail miserably and ruin another. In order to gain expertise, I recommend that you experiment for quite some time before attempting to clean or restore anything you are considering to collect, or offer for sale in your business. In the beginning, I tested various substances and cleaning agents on things I already owned and no longer wanted. Also, I would attempt various methods and techniques on small spots that were hidden or with normal use would not be noticeable. For a nominal amount, I routinely purchased damaged or used items at sales to use as guinea pigs, in order to make a trial run and test the results of various touch-up methods and cleaning agents. Even after painstaking practice and preparation, I have occasionally failed and ruined various effects. Whenever this happens, all you can do is salvage usable parts or pieces that could be adapted for use with other merchandise, and discard the rest. As you are already aware, certain flaws, the surface, or *patina* of some collectibles and antiques, can greatly affect their value. Experts will tell you that some objects gain value: from their use, how they weather, and their age, if they are not altered or damaged. Being able to discern the difference is not easy and should always be left to the experts. Professional dealers and collectors will tell you that original, untouched surfaces add charm, age, and rustic appeal to many objects, whereas cleaning or adding new coat of paint could detract from their appearance, and greatly diminish the value or even render it worthless. Therefore, before you attempt to fix or repair anything, be fully aware of the effect your efforts may have upon the value of the object you are considering for refurbishing. If you are not totally certain of the result, get the experts involved before any trouble occurs. I have seen several segments on the *Antiques Roadshow* where thousands of dollars have been lost when owners clean, paint, or change the finish of their collectibles and antiques. On more than one *Roadshow* episode the value was cut in half and even more.

Most of my cleaning methods were borrowed from *Heloise*, the high priestess of household hints. For over 40 years her family has published a newspaper column with a lot of useful information for cleaning around the house. There is a web site of useful tips at www.heloise.com that you can now access. I have assembled some of my favorite stain removal and cleaning tips for your consideration. First, I must warn you. Amateurs should never attempt to perform *any* cleaning methods or other tips in this book without adequate preparation. Finally, before you try anything on your own property, be certain you fully appreciate the risk, and are prepared to live with the outcome, good or bad.

Miscellaneous Cleaning Tips:

Rust can be removed from metal cookware and other metal objects with cider Vinegar. Put small amount of vinegar on area and after a few minutes pour out. Let stand for a day and rust should disappear.

Stuffed toys can be cleaned with cornstarch if they are not wet or damp. Rub into material and let stand inside a plastic bag overnight. On the following day, shake out the loose powder and brush clean.

Compact Discs can be cleaned with delicate sweeps from an unabrasive cloth *across* the grooves of the disc. A cleaning motion in the same direction as the grooves can damage the disc. Grime or built-up deposits should be carefully washed with running water and dishwashing liquid. Carefully rinse the CD and remove the water with a light shake. Then carefully pat dry with a soft cloth.

Brass when coated with a finish should only be cleaned with water and liquid dishwashing liquid to avoid damage to the finish. All other brass should be washed in soapy water after cleaning with copper or brass cleaner. Then immediately rinse and dry with a soft cloth.

Painted Objects should be cleaned with all-purpose cleaners only after testing on small, less noticeable areas. Do not use cleaners with pine oil that can damage painted surfaces. Also avoid abrasive rubbing of the surface when cleaning and drying.

Wax Removal from containers can be achieved by covering area with hot water and bleach mixture. Let stand for several hours. Repeat the process, if necessary. To remove from carpet or upholstery, place a brown paper bag over the area and pass a hot iron over it. The bag will absorb the wax. On wood, soften wax with hair dryer and remove with paper towel. Clean spot with a vinegar and water solution.

Bakelite has a very delicate finish that can be damaged by rubbing and using alkali or ammonia cleaners. Clean the surface with plain dishwashing liquid (without additives). Deep scratches may be removed by gently polishing with brass cleaner. Remove residue with lighter fluid. *Never use alcohol!* After cleaning, polish with a clean soft, cloth and Armor All.

Surface Scratches on furniture may be filled in or covered up with *Oz Cream Polish.* Follow the directions.

Sticky Glue price tags can be lifted with WD-40 or Goo Gone. Cover the sticky area with the cleaner and wait a minute. You should be able to gently remove the label with your fingernail and then wipe surface clean. Be very careful not to scratch surface when removing tag.

Permanent Marker blemishes can be eliminated from almost anything by using regular plain white toothpaste or mineral spirits.

Blood on fabric or furniture can be dislodged by gently rubbing with hydrogen peroxide. If it is a washable fabric you can also rinse the affected area in cold water and rub in moistened cornstarch. Let dry and brush off.

Marble stains can be cleansed by sprinkling salt on a wedge of fresh lemon. Rub the stain softly to avoid hurting the surface. Then wash with soap and water.

Crayon marks can be removed with toothpaste or ammonia.

Ballpoint Pen marks may be eliminated with alcohol. For stubborn marks, cover area with a clean white cloth and soak for several hours with 3% solution of hydrogen peroxide.

Leather Upholstery can be polished by using a clean cloth and a cream comprised of one part vinegar and two parts linseed oil.

Chrome can be cleaned with club soda or seltzer water.

Book Cleaning Tips:

Moldy Odors can be neutralized by placing book with baking soda overnight in a plastic bag or airtight container. I also heard that kitty litter, coffee, Lysol, fabric softener sheets, and charcoal can be used in the same manner as long as it does not touch the book. For best results, "fan" the book open for maximum exposure.

Gum Eraser will clean dirt from books. Be careful to erase out towards edge of page to avoid tearing.

Cloth Covers can be cleaned with *Absorbene*, a product available in most art supply stores.

Leather Books can be preserved and maintained with application of potassium lactate to binding, followed by dressing of forty percent anhydrous lanolin, and sixty percent neatsfoot oil.

Vellum Bindings can be restored by gently rubbing with milk and cotton wool.

Glossy Surfaces like book jackets will respond to Windex, lighter fluid, or Goo Gone. Put a small amount on a cloth and wipe gently. You can also

GUERILLA GARAGE SALES

remove price stickers with lighter fluid and Goo Gone. Apply to label with napkin or Q-tip and gently remove with fingernail, to avoid scratching the surface.

Bookplates are generally pasted, not glued, so do not attempt any of the above methods. I usually leave the bookplate intact, but if you are determined to remove, only water will work. Cut a piece of absorbent paper to fit the shape of the bookplate, but a little smaller in size. Dampen the paper (do not wet) and place over plate without touching book. Cover with sheet of wax paper, close book, and weight top of book. Wait approximately thirty minutes and it should come off easily.

Crayon Marks can be removed by rubbing affected area with a fine steel wool (0000 grade).

Warning: None of these methods should be attempted on antique or valuable books. Any procedure involving chemicals or highly toxic materials has the potential to damage your valuables. Some stain removal methods may initially appear successful, but could degrade and cause damage over a period of time. You have to be extremely careful whenever you handle chemical products. Always read and follow label directions. Do not forget that if you introduce several substances in succession to work on the same item, you can create a *chemical reaction* that may cause unintended results. Moreover, be safe and always take steps to ventilate your workspace to protect yourself from fumes emanating from cleaning materials that could adversely affect your health. All ingredients are now in place. Remember, trail blazers take most of the arrows.

IX

INTELLIGENCE GATHERING

Correctly assessing and accurately representing the quality of your merchandise is perhaps one of the most important components in marketing products and services to the public. After you compensate for the emotional aspects of buying and selling, the condition of your item is what initially attracts most buyers to your camp. In reality, how you appraise an item may be more important than its actual value and status in attracting potential purchasers.

From the outset there are many ways to grade personal property. I have found that the best way to grade an item is the most straightforward and the least complicated. I try to imagine how I would pitch this item to a sibling or a friend. On those terms maybe the item is not so brand new, and you might not grade it as high. This simple exercise will not only save you considerable grief from unhappy customers, but will help cement your reputation for online honesty and reliability.

This simplistic view is bolstered somewhat by more formal, commercially accepted grading techniques and procedures. Although there are guides out there, for our use, there is no universal grading system for the bulk of the property you will be offering for sale in your business. What is the definition of "grading?" For our purposes, grading is a system to distinguish and rank various items of a similar group or types of property, to determine their physical condition, and ultimately fair value. This type of system is subjective and uniquely dependent on what item is being examined. A practical system for grading books cannot be used in evaluating coins. Therefore, each type of property has its own specific grading method. As a seller, you should educate yourself about the various established

GUERILLA GARAGE SALES

standardized grading systems that are customarily used in a trade or business and try to conform to that system.

Of course, grading the condition of an item is much easier when it is brand new and factory sealed, than when it is used, shopworn, or missing components. Furthermore, depending on the item, different terminology, grading rubrics, and other points of interest will take precedence over others. For example, you would not classify a plasma television as *Very Fine* or a 19th Century Mormon Bible as being *refurbished*. This is because each unique category of goods or collectibles has its own terminology and its own grading standards.

It is not feasible to provide information on every grading system in this space. I will include several common accepted methods you will most likely confront in your business. Based on my own experiences and respectable grading sources in the industry, the following are almost universal grading rubrics for the most popular categories on eBay:

BOOKS

Although I have adapted my own evaluation system for books that I sell, it is still based on the *AB Bookman's 1949 Standard Grading System*, which pioneered the grading condition guidelines for books:

AB BOOKMAN'S GRADING SYSTEM:

As New/Mint (AN or M) is to be used only when the book is in the same immaculate condition in which it was published. There can be no defects, no missing pages, no library stamps, no owner's marks or initials etc., and the dust jacket if it was issued with one must be perfect, without any tears. In summation, it is a copy that is perfect in every respect, including jacket.

Fine (F) approaches the condition of *As New*, but without being crisp. For the use of the term *Fine* there must also be no defects, etc., and if the dust jacket has a small tear, or other defect, or looks worn, this should always be noted.

Very Good (VG) can describe a used book that does show some small signs of wear (but no tears) on either binding or paper. Any defects including owner's marks or initials must be noted.

Good (G) describes the average used and worn book that has all pages or leaves present. Any defects must be noted.

Fair (FR) is a worn book that has complete text pages (including those with maps or plates) but may lack end papers, half-title, etc. (which must be noted). Binding, dust jacket (if any), etc. may also be worn. All defects must still be noted.

Poor (P) describes a book that is so sufficiently worn that its only merit is as a Reading Copy because it does have the complete text, which must be legible. Any missing maps or plates should still be noted. This copy may be soiled, scuffed, stained or spotted and may have loose binding, joints, hinges, pages, etc.

SPECIAL INSTANCES

Moving on to special features of book grading, the following is typically very important to customers and should not be overlooked:

First Edition Except for certain circumstances, the statement of First Edition or First Printing on the copyright page means exactly that—it is a First Edition. However, some publishers use the numerical sequencing system without stating edition, the sequence of numbers is the key to the printing, and one should always be looking for the lowest digit in any sequence, with the numeral "1" being the best. Example: 10 9 8 7 6 5 4 3 2 1...or...1 2 3 4 5 6 7 8 9 10...stands for First Printing of the First Edition, whereas 9 8 7 6 5 4 3...or...3 4 5 6 7 8 9...indicates Third Printing. The key is finding the lowest number to indicate the printing. Also a later, or renewed, copyright date will help enforce the printing sequence.

Autographed Editions are very collectable and can add enormous value to a volume, however, you may have to provide proof to authenticate the signature.

GUERILLA GARAGE SALES

Dust Jacket In all cases, the lack of a dust jacket should be noted. If the book was never issued with one, then state this fact (assume any book published since 1930 included a dusk jacket). If it was manufactured with one but not included you need to report that fact, regardless of the condition of the book. You will have make refunds and receive angry complaints otherwise. If you have a book with no dust jacket and are not confident it was released with one, state it in your ad description.

Ex-library copies must always be designated as such regardless of the book's condition. Library copies are relatively easy to distinguish because they usually have pouches inside the back cover for index cards, are stamped, and have Dewey Decimal System identification numbers written in ink at the bottom of the spine.

Book Club editions must also be noted. You can usually ascertain if a certain book is a book club edition by looking at the title and copyright pages.

Binding Copy describes a book in which the pages or leaves are perfect but the binding is very bad, loose, off, or nonexistent.

Poor (Reading Copy) describes a book so sufficiently worn it only merits a "Reading Copy" status because it does have the complete, legible text. Any missing maps or plates should be noted. This copy may be soiled, scuffed, stained or spotted and may have loose joints, hinges, or pages, but remains intact.

When dealing with collectible or antiquarian books the better practice would be to get them appraised or authenticated by a professional third party until you are qualified. eBay provides the following link for getting professional opinions on books: www.pkbooks.com The link takes you to *PK Books*, which specializes in online book authentication.

CASH HOFFMAN

COINAGE

Based on the Official A.N.A. (American Numismatic Association) Grading Standards for United States Coins:

The grading scale used on American coins is the 70-point scale devised by Dr. William Shelby. On this scale 0 is barely recognizable as a coin and 70 is perfect. Each coin has particular features that will show wear before others.

Mint State (MS) ranges from MS60 to MS70. Shows absolutely no trace of wear.

Almost Uncirculated (AU) ranges from AU50 to AU58. Shows some slight traces of wear on the highest points of the coin.

Extremely Fine (EF) ranges from EF40 to EF45 (sometimes called XF40-XF45). Has light wear on the high points of the coin.

Very Fine (VF) ranges from VF20 to VF35. Shows medium wear on the high points of the coin. All of the major features of the coin are sharp.

Fine (F) ranges from F12 to F15. Has moderate even wear. Some of the detail is worn off.

Very Good (VG) ranges from VG7 to VG10. This grade range is well worn. The major design is there but most of the detail again is worn off.

Good (G) ranges from G4 to G6. This grade range shows heavy wear. The major design is visible but faint in some spots.

About Good (AG) is AG3. Has extremely heavy wear. The date on the coin is visible. Only the outline of the design is visible.

Fair (F) is F2. This grade is worn so heavily that the date may not be easy to make out.

GUERILLA GARAGE SALES

Poor/Basal (P) is P1. This grade is so worn that the only thing you can determine is the type of coin it was.

If you have absolutely no idea how to grade coins, you have no business buying or selling coins without assistance. Grading coinage is not a science but an art. It takes years of experience to make accurate appraisals. Mistakes can be costly when bad press from your customers results in reversals of fortune. Until you are more competent, have an expert grade your coins. eBay provides a link to third parties for this purpose: www.ngccoin.com

The NGC (Numismatic Guaranty Corporation) site gives an independent, expert, and impartial third-party source for your coins' condition. As an added bonus, you will receive a 10% discount if you are an eBay member: www.pcgs.com

The PCGS (Professional Coin Grading Site) provides quality verification and authentication for all American and coins worldwide.

STAMPS

I am not aware of any universal-grading rubric for stamps. Although there are no official rules per se, most philatelists use the following nomenclature and general guidelines to rank stamps by grade, according to *About, Inc.* on *Stamp Grades & Condition*:

> **Superb (S)** the stamp design is perfectly centered on the paper with four large, equal margins. Since this grade is reserved only for unused or mint stamps, there will be no cancellation marks.
>
> **Extremely Fine (XF)** the stamp design is almost perfectly centered with large even margins on all sides. Used stamps will have very light, aesthetically pleasing cancellation marks.
>
> **Very Fine (VF)** stamp design is somewhat off-center but well clear of any of the edges. The margins are still fairly large with no perforations touching the design. Used stamps will have light, neat cancellations.

CASH HOFFMAN

Fine-Very Fine (F-VF) stamp is noticeably off-center on one side, or slightly off-center on two sides. However, the design does not touch any edge and all perforations are well clear of the design. As before, used stamps will have cancellation marks that do not unduly detract from the design.

Average (A) the stamp has the design cutting into two margins of the stamp. Cancellations on used stamps are heavier than normal.

Poor (P) stamp has the design cutting into two or more edges of the stamp. Cancellations are very heavy and detract from (or obliterate) part of the design.

Once again, if you do not know the finer points of stamp collecting, do not estimate the condition or value of a stamp. Grading stamps takes years of practice to achieve accurate results. You should consider guidance from a professional before buying or selling stamps. eBay provides the following links: www.stamps.org

The APS (American Philatelic Society) Expertizing Service offers opinions on the genuineness of philatelic material at moderate cost.

The PSE (Professional Stamp Experts) Stamp Authentication and Grading Site offers authentication and grading services for United States stamps, covers, postal stationery, and Back-of-Book material: www.philatelicfoundation.org

The PF (Philatelic Foundation) site will examine and certify stamps, covers, and other submitted philatelic materials.

CDs, MOVIES/DVDs, VIDEO GAMES

The following is a collaborated list among several sources:

New is what you would expect to see at a store; an item that has never been used or opened. If the item is truly new, this means it should be factory sealed in shrink-wrap. The item should be in pristine condition. There should be no holes or cuts in the barcode or jewel case. The original packaging and all materials are included and are also in brand new condition.

GUERILLA GARAGE SALES

Like New does not mean the item still has to be in shrink-wrap, but it should look like it was just taken out of the shrink-wrap. Item could be played once or twice, but still plays perfectly, with no signs of visual or audio wear either externally or internally. The item is suitable for presenting as a gift.

Very Good means no damage at all to jewel cases or item cover, including scruff marks, scratching, cracks, or holes. A well cared for item that has been played, but remains in great condition. Item plays without interruption, does not skip, and has no fuzzy or snowy frames.

Good has clear external signs of wear, but still continues to play perfectly. Item may have identification markings from its owner. Cases or item cover may show wear.

Acceptable but still continues to play perfectly. Instructions, cases, and item covers may be missing.

Please take notice that every condition designation above states that the item *must play perfectly!* If the item you are selling plays with interruption, skips, or has fuzzy or snowy frames, you will have to specifically state this in the ad description to properly advise the customer. Run that up the flagpole.

X

THE MOST COMMON SNAFU

When grading your wares I must warn you to beware of the most overused term on the Internet describing something for sale—*MINT* (condition). In Roman mythology, the Roman Queen of the Gods was Juno, the daughter of Saturn, wife of Jupiter, and mother of Mars. According to ancient Italian legend, the Goddess Juno warned the Romans through a flock of geese that the Gauls were attacking the Capitolium in 390 B.C. Following that episode, the Romans revered her as *Juno Moneta*. The epithet *moneta* means *to warn* in Latin or *one who makes people remember*. In the ensuing period a temple was dedicated to Juno in her honor at the site of this attack. The first Roman mint was later built nearby and has been producing coins continuously for over 2,000 years. The coins created in this mint became commonly known as *moneta*, which many believe is the root origin of the word *money*. Thus, the word *mint* is associated with an historical omen. For grading purposes it still carries a warning. Use it sparingly and with caution, because it is rare to find an item that is truly in *mint condition*. Accurately grading your merchandise to sell for profit is a key element toward becoming a successful seller on the Internet. Get it right the first time. If you focus only on the good you cannot find the imperfect the buyer will always see.

SECTION TWO:

OPERATING YOUR BUSINESS EFFICIENTLY AND GOOD RECORD KEEPING

I. TIME IS OF THE ESSENCE

There is a legal phrase adopted from English Common Law, which states: *Time is of the essence.* In layman's terms this means that an act must be performed within a certain period of time, or that performance of a contract within or by a specific time is essential in order to complete the agreement of the parties. Therefore, delay is seriously detrimental to the proper fulfillment of an undertaking. In the business world, this concept is expressed as *Time is money*, which denotes time as an essential element, and unless performance is timely, it will likely lead to a loss. In other words, procrastination costs. It is a natural human response to often withhold task performance because we do not want to deal with things right away. Simply stated, you need to maximize your time and place a value on it, to be successful. Now is more crucial. On garage sale day, every minute you spend outside of acquiring new merchandise for your business is unproductive, and ultimately may adversely affect your bottom line. Like a heat-seeking missile, I usually infiltrate fifteen garage sales in approximately three hours time. You have to be highly organized and mechanized to accomplish your mission. Additionally, if your merchandise is lying on the shelf and has not been listed on the web, you have no opportunity of recouping your costs or earning a profit. And, the value of your merchandise may be depreciating and becoming less valuable lying around. Likewise, one needs to value his time in pursuing this enterprise. For example, if you spend one hour producing one Ebay ad for a two-dollar item, is this the most productive use of your time? Before you undertake any task,

81

always ask yourself: "Is the reward worth it?" It takes about an equal amount of time to list a $50.00 item. In the final analyses, don't forget that time *is* money, money you'll never get back. Never lose sight of it! The English poet, *Edward Young* called procrastination "the thief of time." Every minute you waste in unproductive activity necessitates an opportunity loss. The message is clear. The world is turning.

II

CONDITION, CONDITION, CONDITION

A wise person well versed in the real estate market once said that there are only three things that are important in the sale of a piece of real estate—location—location—location. In this business the *condition* of your merchandise is the single most critical element. Everything revolves around how your item is graded and sold by you. I will cover grading later on, but the price you receive is generally higher, the better the condition of your product. Moreover, your customers do not necessarily grade the same way you do. What I do to avoid problems from the outset, is grade down i.e., I generally rate the item a little lower on the quality scale, or slightly overemphasize minor weaknesses or minute faults of the product. This works very well. Most of my customers are usually satisfied, because many vendors grade up, and disappoint expectations. Furthermore, I sometimes throw in extras for goodwill. Oftentimes when I buy in bulk I may pick up smaller items of minimal value that I cannot sell individually. Rather than discard or donate them, I purposely add them to orders at no extra charge and the effect on customers is dramatic. For example I sold a large number of *GOOSEBUMPS* books for a child. I included a small GOOSEBUMPS toy in the order at no extra charge. I really had no cost in the toy, but the customer was very appreciative. This buyer became a repeat customer and purchased several other items from me. I also use this extra value technique if there has been a less than perfect order, and it helps smooth over problems with customers. Anything you can do toward developing goodwill with your customers will bring you future rewards. It seems to me that many vendors do not go this extra mile. You will definitely make a favorable impression that makes a powerful statement on your behalf if you routinely utilize some form of this business practice. Most businesses operate under the assumption that you try to satisfy your customer. Satisfaction entails providing goods for which you have already been paid, and service at a level the customer already expects. The most successful enterprises strive to go beyond the expected and provide something extra for their purchaser that is not expected. The buying public will remember this and value doing business with you. Build a reservoir of goodwill and make it an integral part of your business strategy. You must set the standard to which all others should be compared. Otherwise, "If you do things the way they've always been done, you'll get what you've always got."—*Jack Welch*

III

PURCHASE FOR YOUR OWN HQ

Besides making money directly from the sale of garage sale items, you can also save money by buying supplies and products for yourself as you maneuver the weekend war. I have picked up all kinds of office supplies, photographic equipment, and other business equipment that I needed and used in my business, for pennies on the dollar. I have acquired computer software, a color printer, printer cartridges, writing materials, envelopes, and paper products for invoices and record keeping. I have found packing materials, storage shelving, storage bins, and other shipping and mailing products useful in my day-to-day operation. In addition, I have even found brand new computer hardware components to upgrade my PC at very reasonable prices. If you are in no hurry to secure stock and are constantly on the lookout, you can find almost everything that you need of good quality at most garage sales, to conduct your business at unbelievably low cost to you. Any good commando knows how to live off the land. You can too! Use this avenue of commerce as a valuable resource to help in the battle against rising costs, run your business efficiently, and minimize your expense of operation at the same time. Your business will be the ultimate beneficiary. When you hit the target the caliber of the bullet does not matter.

IV

BE ALL YOU CAN BE

My parents grew up in the Age of Aquarius—LOVE, PEACE, FLOWER POWER, and VIETNAM. We live in the New Millennium, the Age of Specialization. Doctors, lawyers, and other professionals routinely secure board certification to practice in one particular area of expertise. Hobbyists and collectors generally confine the object of their affections to a particular collectible or item. A large number of businesses cater to a single product or service, or a small number of merchandise categories in their product line. A *caveat* to the wise however—market conditions go up and down and can be a roller coaster at times. Diversification is always the best defense to a slumping market or a product line that may fall into disfavor in the market place. Find a niche that you can fill. The reason for this is obvious. It is considerably less difficult and more productive to devote one's time and resources to a small number of stock items. As a tactical guerilla specialist, you can concentrate your efforts and acquire expertise in a shorter period of time. There are fewer publications to review, a smaller number of product shows to attend, and time spent on marketing and selling is significantly reduced. Shipping and handling costs are less because of the uniform requirements of distribution associated with limited inventory.

Moreover, there is an added bonus if you choose a commercial pursuit that you already enjoy and have some knowledge. What do you think has been the number one sales commodity of all time—information! Personally, I have always loved reading. As a young child, I acquired good reading skills naturally and nurtured a strong appreciation for the printed word. As I grew older, I moved beyond accelerated reading and matured into the bibliophile that I am today. In seventh grade, my middle school had an annual accelerated reading competition. The reader amassing the most accelerated reader points

GUERILLA GARAGE SALES

by the end of the contest got to be "Principal For A Day." In addition to that dubious distinction, the overall contest winner and three of his friends were treated to pizza—on the house—after being chauffeured to the restaurant in a limousine! My friends and I still reminisce the day I was awarded this special commendation.

As my online business has successfully developed, I still enjoy reading. So, it was a natural thing for me to specialize in books. There are also some obvious benefits associated with ownership and certain perks for book lovers. You get to read the merchandise, then sell it, buy more...read...sell...*ad infinitum*. Books are easy to store, do not demand a massive amount of space, and are suited to most living quarters in holding for resale. Unless you delve into antique or rare books, one does not normally have to infuse large sums of cash for their acquisition, which is a plus if you have limited capital to invest. Most sales have some books, even if they are not advertised. There is a robust market for books and you rarely have to hold them for a long period of time before they ultimately sell. Furthermore, books are easy to ship and do not require any special handling or packaging requirements. We are reminded that: "so long as a book may be opened the mind will never be closed."

The number one reason I am sold on this subject is that that our Government encourages the dissemination of books, writings, and certain other electronic media. By act of Congress, the U.S. Postal Service has had a longstanding stake in such publications, and has continually subsidized their distribution. I am specifically referring to "Media Mail." Long ago the United States Congress made a conscious decision that it was a worthy endeavor to promote the dissemination of ideas, art, and educational materials. Not long ago, the mailing of books was commonly shipped by a very preferential "book rate," which was a very low postal fee charged for mailing such items." Presently we have the new category of "Media Mail," which is essentially the same animal as its precursor, but its benefits extend to more than books. Under the United States Postal Service guidelines, small and large parcels can be mailed under this subheading. Contents are limited to..."books, manuscripts, sound recordings, recorded videotapes, and computer-readable media (not blank)...Media Mail cannot contain advertising, except books can contain incidental announcements of other books."

In rare instances one might take advantage of another limited shipping option available from the Post Office—"Bound Printed Matter." Permanently bound printed materials are essentially "advertising, promotional materials, directory materials, and editorial materials" of 15 pounds or less. There is a major disadvantage to Bound Printed Material shipping. If delivery fails for any reason, the item will *not* be returned to the shipper unless the shipper guarantees the return postage. This return language must be printed conspicuously on the package.

Various congressmen and postal officials confirm that from its very infancy, book rate/media mail has consistently lost money most every year of its existence. This monetary shortfall has been compensated by the bulk of all other postal revenue categories handled by the United States Postal Service and the General Revenue Fund of the United States Government. But the steadfast belief remains—the benefits of free and unfettered publication of unregulated thoughts, ideas, speech, and educational communication, fostered by this uniquely American institution, far outweigh the loss of revenue. And, the shipping costs associated with Media Mail are extremely low, when compared to every other mailing/shipping category offered by the Post Office, or any other carrier delivery system in this country. Regardless of where you live, the following website is exceptionally useful in locating book sales: http://www.booksalefinder.com/. This site includes both USA and Canadian calendars of book sales. There is also contact information, locations, and details of sales, most of which offer hundreds of thousands of books at a single event! Finally, a very in depth source for many questions and general information about books can be found at http://www.massmedia.com/~mikeb/rcb/. This reference covers a multitude of topics, such as identifying a first edition, autographs, how to tell if a book was issued with a dust jacket, and much more. There are hundreds of frequently asked questions about the "care and feeding of books." The best intelligence information is useless if you do not use it.

V

RECYCLE AND LIVE OFF THE LAND

One environment, one chance to care for it—YOU can save the earth!

It is imprudent to operate a business today without taking into account waste reduction and cost elimination. In fact, if a company does not successfully handle these objectives, their continued operation is at risk. According to the Environmental Protection Agency, in the year 2000, paper and paperboard made up the largest component of municipal solid waste at 37%. The amounts of municipal solid waste generated and recycled have changed considerably over the last few decades. Waste generation has increased drastically over the decades. EPA records indicate that in 1960 the generation rate was 2.7 pounds/person/day. In 1980 the rate was 3.7 pounds/person/day. In 1990 the rate was 4.5 pounds/person/day and this is where it has stabilized. However, recycling rates have also increased in the past three decades from 10% in 1980 to 16% in 1990 and finally 30% in 2000.

At this moment, small businesses across the United States are recycling millions of tons of trash a year. Even the operation of a small mail order/internet business like mine lends itself to many recycling opportunities. For example, I have *never purchased a shipping container and I never will!* From the onset of my business operation, I have been able to scrounge from the trash every box, Styrofoam protector, packing peanut, plastic bag, bubble wrap, cardboard divider, and all invoice/record/shipping paper products that I have ever needed. To date, I have stockpiled several years worth of these materials for the future. I owe much to my friends, family, individuals, and other businesses who save these materials for me. Nonetheless, I personally retrieve large contingents of my shipping materials from refuse containers. I have certain strategic locations that I routinely check for these packing and shipping supplies. I only "dumpster dive" in receptacles that are relatively

89

clean and are primarily filled with paper and paperboard refuse. I avoid containers that discard food, chemicals, hazardous waste, or other messy, wet garbage. And, of course, I do not actually physically insert myself into the trash container. It did not take long for me to get control of my shipping requirements. I learned how to load up on free material and how to store it for future use. Boxes can be broken down and easily stored flat until needed. All other packing products can be stored in large plastic leaf bags and placed out of harms way in your attic. Finally, everyone in our family recycles all leftover packaging materials from shipments to our home, along with the containers and packaging from everyday shopping and purchases that we make during the year. I also utilize these raw materials to ship merchandise to my customers. Moreover, I recycle used printer cartridges and old cell phones. *Office Max* (if there is one near you) will trade one ream of copier paper for one cartridge or one cell phone.

There is another form of recycling that actually surprised me when I was first introduced to it. Once I began reusing discarded "trash" and "junk" that other people no longer wanted, I realized there was *nothing wrong with many things people literally throw away every day!* It is an ancient and antiquated idea about one man's trash being someone else's treasure, but I can honestly attest to the absolute truth of this maxim. I have found money in the trash can! I have found a host of other types of property including antiques, writing implements, wine opener, games, lamps, furniture, furnishings, household items, cookware, toys, music, fixtures, collectibles, electronics, personal items, books and magazines, wearing apparel, copper and aluminum scrap, and much more than I can list. Many of these items were unused or factory sealed in their original packaging. On numerous occasions during the year after a successful recycling excursion," I have taken items to my quarters and listed them online. Most of the time this "trash" or "junk" sells for a handsome profit. Recycling is more than putting plastic milk jugs and aluminum cans in a container. The heart of recycling is the actual re-use of resources in their present state, instead of collecting and sending materials like paper, plastic, and glass to the factory to fashion new products. This is another business challenge that we need to meet squarely and use the same entrepreneurship and innovation that we employ in every other area of operation. Remember that the best way to keep profits up is to keep costs down. Now, to my way of thinking that is big money. In conclusion, admittedly there is a social stigma associated with coming in contact with "garbage", but if you are willing to get your hands a little dirty, trash pays. Never be too busy to stop and smell the garbage. Recycling works! *Recycle today so tomorrow won't go to waste.*

VI

PROTECT YOUR FORCE

If the typical garage sale host is not a businessman, you can surely say the same thing for the average Internet buyer. Therefore, what would the impact on your business be, if you could earn additional income on approximately five per cent of your sales without necessarily incurring additional costs or loss of time? How would you like a profit windfall? I am referring to a calculated business risk you may consider taking by *being your own shipping insurer*. It is commonly referred to as "self-insurance." If, for example, you sell someone a $5.00 book and your profit margin is $4.00, your earnings would be considerably healthier if you could realize an additional $1.30 on the same sale. Do the math. That additional income amount is the cost of insuring an item of $100.00 or less via the United States Post Office. Why someone would pay this amount and insure a $5.00 book is beyond the scope of this discussion—but they do. They also insure numerous other things of minimum value, which are not likely to be damaged or lost in shipment. I have not calculated the probability or exact odds of loss in these situations, but they must be considerably low. In guerilla terms, it is an acceptable risk management technique. I do know I have *only paid* for three lost or damaged items since I began utilizing this operational method. I have heard from other vendors who claim their probable loss range is three to five items per thousand. My loss ratio experience to date after surpassing 8,500 transactions has been less than that. This means by the time you may have to pay for a loss, you have collected on so many transactions that you are money ahead and can easily afford to pay for an occasional loss out of your own pocket. Not too shabby, not too shabby indeed! Because we live in the real world, it is safe to conclude that there is some risk, but that risk is manageable if you apply it reasonably. Further, you are already standing behind everything that you sell anyway if they are shipped without insurance, because the buyer is going to come back to you with any problems. Occasionally I hedge my bet by purchasing delivery confirmation from the Post Office. It costs fifty cents and allows you to prove delivery only. Obviously, you would not want to use the self-insurance option in every transaction. When and if you decide to exercise the courage of your convictions is up to you. Always remember: If you want to win in this war, you have to fight differently.

The other side of the coin is that in a perfect world there are nothing but profits, there are no losses, and love is always true. As we are all aware, this is not a perfect world, far from it. Sometimes a buyer may actually receive an item but report it as lost. Therefore, when you assume the risk and anything untoward happens, you will have to stand behind the sale. This means that *you* become the insurance company warranting the value of the goods and any potential loss. The bottom line is you will be financially responsible to the buyer up to the full amount of his purchase. Another note, you reimburse the cost of the damaged or lost item, not the shipping costs. Finally, your reputation is everything. *Henry Ford* once said: "you can't build a reputation on what you are going to do." Unless you are just as willing to write a check to settle a claim, as quickly as you expect payment from a buyer for a sale, do not consider this method. Do the math and make a calculated business decision. And remember, those who live by the sword usually get shot by those who don't.

VII

ASSESSMENT AND COMMAND INFORMATION

Decision-making is the most important managerial function. If you have never operated a business, one of the biggest tactical command decisions a guerilla specialist will most likely ponder—is deciding what to charge for goods or services. Select a high price and no one will buy from you. Charge too little and you may not make a profit. Even if you earn a profit your enterprise could still fail if your profit margin is too thin. You always want to sell at the highest price, but how? Price is a number that you can quantify, but it involves other non-numerical factors such as product availability, its function, and other attributes. To compound this dilemma, any item is ultimately only worth what someone is willing to pay for it. Further, online selling is extremely competitive because there is more of it, and it is worldwide. Because of increased global competition, no one ever wants to pay you what something is truly worth—they want to pay as little as possible! They want and expect a bargain every time they go online, just like you do when you go to a garage sale.

There are mathematical formulas to aid your pricing decisions. The simplest pricing formula is Price = Cost + Profit. The price you will charge is your reasonable profit margin plus costs. Therefore, before you can set your price, you need to know the *full cost* of purchasing and owning a given item for sale. Costs generally fall into three categories: direct, labor, and indirect (overhead). Direct costs are those expenses associated with acquisition or manufacture of the products you are selling. In other words, if you buy a finished product—what you pay the supplier for an item that you intend to re-sell is the *direct cost*. Likewise, if you manufacture a product, the price you pay for raw materials or components to produce the item, is the

93

direct cost. *Labor costs* include all wages and benefits you pay employees, including your own account. You should include your own salary whether you draw it or not, because your time has value. And if you fail to value your time, you are working for nothing. *Indirect cost*, or *overhead*, is everything else you pay to operate your business such as rent, supplies, equipment, postage and shipping, insurance, professional services, utility costs, and the like. The easiest way to increase profits is to raise prices, but you have to be careful. The market may not bear a higher price, and you can lose competitive advantage if your prices are not within the range customers are willing to pay. Another way to raise profits is to increase sales, but this is not always the best strategy because when sales increase the costs associated with your business have to be expended upward. Usually the most difficult alternative, reducing costs, is the most cost-effective strategy for increasing income. When you reduce your overhead every dollar you make you get to keep. Thus, the best way to increase price is to reduce expenses and costs of operation, unless you want to reduce your profit margin.

There is an old saying in business: *No one was ever ruined by taking a profit*. That adage may be true, but merely focusing on profit margins alone is no guarantee of success or staying power in business. Clearly if you do not make a profit you will not continue in business for very long, but to be successful and continue operations, you have to earn more money than you spend. Thus, sales merchandise must be priced to provide a sufficient "mark-up" or margin, so that a businessman can cover all costs of business, and realize a net profit. Ultimately, the price you charge to sell a product has to be low enough to attract buyers and make a sale, and high enough to maintain a reasonable profit margin to remain in business. And, there cannot be profits unless you cover *all* expenses of operation. Moreover, you spend something more valuable than money in business—time. And we all know that time is money. Setting prices can be tricky because there are several price standards to consider.

SUGGESTED RETAIL PRICE

The first pricing method to consider as a new online business, is the retail or *suggested retail price* (SRP) quoted by the manufacturer. This price is the minimum "suggested" price for which a product may be sold to the public, not the maximum price. Federal fair trade laws provide that merchants can sell their goods at whatever price they choose, as long as they do not conspire

GUERILLA GARAGE SALES

with others similarly situated to illegally set prices. Further, under the law, manufacturers and distributors of products are allowed to quote a suggested price to their merchants and retail distributors, who, in turn may ignore the suggestion, and charge whatever they feel is justified. This is the spirit of the law, but in practice this rarely happens. In the real world, if merchants and retailers ignore the suggested retail price of their supplier and sell below the SRP, they will shortly be unable to purchase any additional inventory from their distributors and brand owners. Pricing goods in business is a double-edged sword. Manufacturers and suppliers of goods are free to do business with whomever they select, but if you do not march to their tune, they will find another unit to conduct joint operations. The reverse of this is also true. Retail establishments can choose their inventory suppliers, but it may be more difficult for retailers to find other suppliers of inventory when they disregard suggested pricing. The point is this: if you buy directly from manufacturers and distributors, they may have some input into your pricing, and control to some extent how you sell their products. The reason for this dichotomy is that brand holders must have the right to protect the integrity of their brands. Finally, the suggested retail price is usually the highest price an item will bring at sale. In my experience, I rarely sell items in my business at the suggested retail price. Most of my sales transactions revolve around second hand goods with price tags below SRP. On occasion, however, I sell merchandise at or above the suggested retail price. I achieve this pricing level in instances when I am selling a brand new item with high consumer demand or an older product in great demand but limited supply. I am also able to retail price when a buyer resides in an isolated area without access to conventional retail outlets, the buyer has other limited shopping options in his area, or he may demand special delivery or other services not available to him from brick and mortar retailers. You may determine a retail price on Web sites such as:

www.pricewatch.com
www.pricescan.com
shopping.yahoo.com

The Federal Trade Commission regulates all commercial activity in this country, on land, "sea" (not really), and in the air, including the Internet. If anyone has a consumer problem, all they have to do is contact the FTC by calling 1-877-FTC-HELP (382-4357 or file a complaint on their web site at (http://www.ftc.gov. This agency does not assist individual consumers, but can take action against a company if there is a history of wrongdoing. For individual assistance, contact your state Attorney General's office.

COMPETITIVE PRICE

Another common method to evaluate for your business is *competitor pricing*. There will be numerous other sellers like you in the marketplace offering the same items or comparable items you have for sale. Therefore, you must realize from the outset that you are not inventing the wheel and are by no means isolated in this global sea of commerce. Accordingly, from time to time on a regular basis, one should monitor pricing and promotional activities of the competition to see how you compare. This does not mean to develop a strategy to routinely undersell the competition at every opportunity, or set prices based solely on the competition. You should merely check out competitors and other sellers. Compare what they are doing, appropriate their methods, ideas, and customize them to suit your needs. If you are able, get their advice, solicit it, and avoid their mistakes. And, if possible, team up with them whenever it is advantageous to you.

Price does not always equal price, however. Your competitor's price may not be what it seems if you fail to add on all other costs, fees, and packaging. Although shoppers are primarily concerned with price in the marketplace, other more important considerations may overshadow the individual prices you may charge. Business tenure, quality control, shipping, service after the sale, your company's business reputation, and other quantifiable factors can make or break a sale just as easily. The lowest bidder does not necessarily always get the job when contracts are let for public and private bid. Would you fly on an airplane that was manufactured by the lowest bidder, and the only consideration for obtaining the contract was price? Before taking off in the wild blue yonder, I would want to know how long this company has been in business, how many airplanes they have built, what is their service and safety record, how their product compares with others in the industry, and other similar considerations. From my experience, if your product or service is identical to your competitor, this usually poses no problems in the pricing department, just charge what the market already supports, and be more concerned about service, quality, and reputation. By way of example, I often find myself surrounded by other sellers who have products for sale that are identical or comparable to mine. My price may be the same as theirs or even a little higher, but I ultimately close the sale. This happens to me too often to be a coincidence. Obviously then, the buyer considers more than price in making his purchase decision, or I would be out of business. In a nutshell, you should develop a pricing structure at or below your competition, as well as buy low and sell high. In other words, half of your success is tied to what you pay for your inventory. Buy it as cheaply as possible and sell it for the best price you can obtain. And, operate your business in such a manner that price is not the most important consideration, but keep an eye on the competition. Of course you will never be able to sell everything you acquire at your ideal price. Be prudent and clear out stale merchandise, by selling off inventory at or below cost to recoup your capital investment in order to purchase new inventory and restart the business cycle. Even when you are pruning out the dead wood, shoppers may buy more profitable items from you, so never take your eye off marketing your merchandise. However, you cannot continue to reduce prices all the way to prosperity. Whether or not you went to business school all other things being equal, the supplier with the lowest cost usually makes the sale.

INTERNET AUCTION PRICE

Auctions have spread into the mainstream at a rapid pace since 1995, beginning with the rise of the Internet. The entire philosophy of Internet auction pricing is different from retail pricing. This hot modern phenomenon is the outgrowth and natural evolution in cyberspace of the old "open-cry" or English auction, with which most people are familiar. Regardless of whether you are looking for a treasure to buy, or thinking about selling the "junk" from your attic to make extra income, this is a wonderful time in which we live to do business. Recent figures are overwhelming—over 36.5 million Americans have participated in online auctions, which is 31% of the U.S. Internet population. Price statistics contained in many accepted economic treatises relating to traditional English auctions, correlate very closely with market pricing set by Internet auctions. The *Auction Price* is theoretically the "true" or correct market price which accurately reflects the quality of the merchandise offered for sale in a free market arena where all participants have complete knowledge of all material facts, and act accordingly. With an auction there is no guesswork or formulas to consider when selling your products—the market sets the price above the minimum selected by the seller to begin the sale. Auction-based pricing is sometimes called "*dynamic*" or "*fluid*" pricing, in contrast to set or static pricing models. However, many believe that the Internet auction price is closer to the true price than the traditional auction model. There are several reasons for this view. The Internet offers a *"virtual flea market "*that removes several stumbling blocks that have continually hampered traditional open-cry auctions. Barriers to participating online are minimal and make it more popular every day. Also, the ease of Internet commerce is a huge difference. E-hubs allow an unlimited number of potential buyers and sellers, (literally millions from around the world), to gather "virtually" on any given site on the web where practically anyone can trade practically anything. This eliminates tremendous costs associated with conducting a traditional auction, as well as the ease of bringing buyers and sellers together to conduct business and establish the true market price. The Internet has made time and geography irrelevant. Because the Internet never closes, commerce is conducted globally 24 hours a day, seven days a week, all year long. For example, Ebay has an established customer base in 90 countries. Moreover, you can buy and sell at 3:00 o'clock in the morning or any other time during the day or night—even while most people sleep! Therefore, because of the unlimited number of "cyber-auction" transactions that occur more frequently on the web, the established Internet price is more likely to be the true price for a particular item. Using eBay as an example, there are several auction-pricing formats to consider, and there are several varieties and permutations of each model you can employ on the Internet:

1.   Dutch Auctions. Are utilized when Seller has several of the same items of like kind and quality. The seller can choose a fixed price for each, or sell them individually by auction.

2.   Buy it Now. Item is listed at a stated beginning price, but buyer has option to end auction immediately at a higher stated price. However, if anyone starts the bidding at lower bid amount, the "Buy it Now" option disappears and the normal auction format is utilized toward conclusion of sale. If a lower bid is posted and the auction continues, bidding can surpass the higher "Buy it Now" price.

3.   Fixed-Price Format. Bidder pays immediately set price offered by Seller without auction.

GUERILLA GARAGE SALES

4.   Reserve Price Auctions. Seller picks lowest price (which is usually not disclosed) he will accept to sell. If no one reaches minimum price, the sale ends and Seller retains goods. Buyers are usually "put off" by reserve bidding. There is a trend where Sellers publish the reserve price in the body of their ad. In this way, the Seller has the minimum price protection, and the Buyer does not have to play games to arrive at a bid.

5.   Proxy Bidding. Buyer chooses highest bid they would offer and eBay continues bidding in increments on Buyer's behalf until bid is won or Buyer is outbid.

Each of the above auction models has other rules, restrictions, and fees governing its use. Further, you can choose the lengths of time best suited to run your auction under any of these formats. On eBay you can select 3-, 5-, 7-, or 10-day periods to conduct your sale.

Marketing is in ferment. It is a discipline that is ever evolving. Selling "cheap" is not marketing. Traditional advertising is in decline and buyers are becoming savvy about the marketplace. Like most fundamental rules of business however, the laws of economics are just as relevant in cyberspace. You can play with them; you can manipulate them; but you cannot change them. To succeed in business you have to know and follow these rules and respect your competition. When you sell you want more of it; you can't get enough. Define your objectives and act accordingly.

VIII

KILL THEM WITH KINDNESS

The one thing that will hurt your business more than anything is *bad service*. It has been said there are no original ideas in the world any more; everything has been thought of at least once before, and we merely rediscover them. A passage in the Bible pronounced over two thousands of years ago: "there is nothing new under the sun." Good service, everybody knows that—even *Moses* understood the concept. Saying it is not doing it, however. If you are not truly committed to this line of thinking you will fail in your business objective. You *must:* respond quickly and positively to all communications; ship quickly and professionally; make certain that the item is properly packaged and addressed; and provide a quality product as advertised. In today's marketplace, customer patience is extremely limited. The speed of business demands instant consumer fulfillment as consumers continue to look for quick solutions for their on-the-go lifestyles. The buying public will not wait for you, or give you many opportunities to fulfill their business expectations before they move on to the next guy in uniform. And, it is more difficult to find another customer than re-sell to the one you already have. It takes years to build up a customer base, but you can lose them in an instant after a minor skirmish. A lost customer is nearly impossible to get back and very expensive to replace. Besides customer attrition, substandard service could affect your reputation to the point it might retard acquisition of new customers. Your attitude can make or break you in dealing with your customers. Be honest and do not mislead them. Earn their business and respect—and keep it! Service is crucial to continued growth. You cannot provide too much service. Sometimes too much is exactly right, if it makes you stand out—one of the few, the proud...

Good service does not simply happen by accident, and it does not happen overnight. It has to be an integral part of your marching orders. Above all else, you have to maintain the same service level when you are not feeling well or you would rather be doing something else...even when the customer is wrong, rude, impolite, or difficult to communicate with. When this happens, I remember the service motto I strive to live by, and I *kill 'em with kindness.*

This is my motto and *I mean it:*

A CUSTOMER:

◎   is not dependent on me, I am dependent on him
◎   is not an interruption of my work, he is the purpose of it
◎   is doing a favor by letting me serve his needs
◎   is not an outsider to my business, he is a part of it

—UNKNOWN

When you communicate your desire to serve, the public will test your resolve. Be prepared to deliver fully and completely on your service commitment. Serving the public is often an arduous, thankless job. Even if your performance is stellar it seems like the complaints you receive often outnumber the kudos. One of my first complaints came from a customer who had purchased a book from me. She stated in her e-mail that she felt that the book I sold her was "very good" and not in "like new" condition as I had advertised—what was I going to do about it? It was a ten-dollar item. In actuality I knew there was nothing wrong with the condition of the book. I had a difficult customer on my hands. Rather than debating the merits of her complaint and going downhill from there, I immediately took the high ground and replied: that "I regretted the inconvenience, I would gladly make an adjustment on the sale, or refund her purchase price if she was not satisfied with the transaction." I ended by once again apologizing for any difficulty this may have caused and asked her to let me know what she wanted me to do to fulfill her service needs. The entire tone of her next e-mail reply changed. She stated that she honestly liked the book and it really was not that bad after all. She ended by saying she wanted to keep it and forget everything. Ultimately, she gave me positive feedback. What I learned from this transaction and later ones like it that occasionally occur, is that the public will frequently test you to ascertain if you are sincere in your business promises and other stated policies. In other words, do you practice what you preach? Sometimes things go wrong. When you receive complaints, apologize first, and address the problem *immediately*. Resolve it quickly and positively, rather than waiting for the perfect moment that never comes. The natural human tendency is to avoid problems but this will only reinforce the customer's belief that you are not sincere in your policies and they are correct in their unreasonable demands. Customers are quicker to scold than to praise; it is human nature. Why do people make a big deal out of small problems? For one thing, it is only one sale to you, but this is the *only sale* to your customer, therefore it is a big deal to that person. The customer may not always be right, but it is better for you to take that position because you will ultimately benefit. *Marshall Field* said "right or wrong, the customer is always right" because he can spend his hard-earned money elsewhere. In the long run it is always better to save one's integrity than a few dollars. Always cheerfully offer to refund their money if they are not satisfied unless they have crossed the line and are attempting to take extreme advantage of you. Do not let a customer's demands take control of your business. Be courteous and apologetic, try to ascertain why they were not satisfied, and learn from it. It is better to take a small loss on one sale than receive negative feedback affecting future sales. You must carefully evaluate each instance and decide the proper course. And, if you handle it properly, you might not have a loss at all. Each customer you serve may have a different need. If there is not a solution to fit that need, you must find one. See your business as a process of constant improvement and customer service. No matter how long you stay in business, customer service never grows old. You've got to dare to be great, dare to challenge, dare to win.

IX

MAXIMIZE YOUR COMMUNICATIONS ARRAY

In Texas we have a saying about a segment of the population who is difficult to please: *Some people wouldn't be happy if you hung 'em with a new rope*. You know who I am talking about—people who want something for nothing—people who expect everything and give very little in return—people who push the envelope and *are difficult by nature*. If you are going to survive this war financially, you are going to have to maintain operational readiness, information superiority, and strike preemptively. I have provided guidelines for customer service, grading, and product quality. Another increasing popular marketing consideration is the technical wording, product features, and other details of your sales ad and customer communications. The Four Corners of your ad and all other customer communication must be very specific, clear, and concise in describing your products. *Never assume* anything or leave room for doubt when you communicate with the public. Predictably, the mind-set of the buyer is that he will always assume everything in his favor—to your detriment. If your sales copy does not specifically rule out a possibility, the buyer will take the position, in most instances, that it is *included* as an integral part of the sale. Let me illustrate the problem. About two years ago I purchased several pallets of sporting goods and other stores. Included in the lot were some 100 new gun scopes and other sighting devices for assorted small arms. I was not well informed on these munitions in advance. I read the enclosed literature and tried to familiarize myself with each item before I listed them for sale on eBay. My first sale to a single purchaser included ten "red dot" scopes for side arm target acquisition. These are infrared sighting devices that help illuminate the target. My ad was complete and drafted directly from the product literature.

I listed all of the features and specifications of each item, straight from the box and enclosed paperwork. I also delineated exactly what parts and accessories were included in the sale, down to the original box, Allen wrench for installation, instructions, and cleaning cloth. Since they were not included, I did not list batteries in the body of my ad. However, I did not specifically state the magic words: *"batteries not included!"* Predictably, the buyer took a different position. In the end I provided $100.00 worth of batteries after the sale which destroyed my profit margin. Furthermore, I learned another lesson the hard way; when batteries are provided—protect yourself with the disclaimer: *battery life not guaranteed,* or similar notification to the purchaser in advance of the sale, or you will be called upon to replace them —I guarantee it!

Another memorable learning experience presented itself when I sold an expensive Nikon camera for a client. Selling for more than fifteen hundred dollars, this was a "big ticket" item. Besides covering the special shipping and handling features of this sensitive instrument, I attempted to protect my financial return on this sale by limiting the buyer's payment options. There are commercial entities like PayPal, who serve as a financial intermediary between the parties. In order to finalize a transaction quickly and receive prompt shipment, the buyer will provide his credit card payment directly to PayPal or some other company. PayPal, a recognized leader in the industry, provides guaranty of payment to the Seller, who ships the order immediately after the funds are transferred electronically to his account—less a handling fee *PAID BY THE SELLER, NOT THE BUYER.* The fee is based upon a percentage of the sales price. When I prepared this camera ad, the payment options included only the following: "check, certified funds, or wire transfer." I did this to avoid a considerable charge to my account by commercial transactional providers, like PayPal. Believe it or not, a small detail presented a problem following this sale. The buyer agreed that I did not specifically list PayPal as a payment option, but he maintained that my ad still contained the PayPal logo, and this was misleading. After that transaction I had to temporarily remove this type of logo from my ad whenever I desired deletion of this payment method. A similar dispute arose when I sold an empty cigar box, but failed to disclaim *thanks, but no cigars.* Would you assume cigars were included in this sale? This buyer did. People do not do what you expect; they do what you inspect.

I am not a JAG lawyer, but I am beginning to think like one when it comes to my business. For instance, when I sell leather products, I include a large

GUERILLA GARAGE SALES

written NOTICE in the cargo container, that such items require special handling treatment and should never be stored in plastic bags. I also recommend consultation with professionals specializing in leather goods before attempting self-cleaning. State the obvious in your ad. Even though the picture of the book you are selling clearly does not have a dust jacket, just say it in your ad copy, or someone may call your hand and cost you money. Remember that good communication was not invented one day and is waiting to be rediscovered—it must be continually invented and reinvented every day in your business. It often seems like those with the least commitment in life make the most demands on others. You can plug a hole, but somebody will go and drill another one.

X

DEFINE YOUR MISSION

Every enterprise has a purpose, a reason for being. To be successful, you need to be crystal clear on your mission, goal attainment, and the direction of your force. Who are you? What are you trying to achieve? How will you battle competitors? What is your strategic vision for acquiring and maintaining a customer base? These and other threshold questions must be the core of an effective mission statement. Initially, most entrepreneurs fantasize about being Number One. They feel they are primed to crush the competition, customers will literally flock to their doorstep, and they intend to make a million dollars over night...but this is before enthusiasm cools, and promise soon collides with reality. This is why you need a plan in advance—a mission statement.

Moreover, it is not realistic to espouse everything you expect to achieve in your mission statement, but it starts the process, allowing you to express and communicate your values, aim high, and set realistic goals. A good mission statement is more like a blueprint of your key goals at the start of your business, with a dose of reality thrown in. It is a roadmap of milestones to be achieved in the future, and briefly how you intend to achieve them, utilizing a few short sentences—with every word weighted equally. At the very least a comprehensive mission statement should answer three questions about your business and its work that translate into: (1) Who you are, and what is the purpose of your organization; (2) the direction and key strategies for reaching goals and addressing needs; and (3) the values that distinguish you from competitors. Furthermore, your mission can evolve. This initial assertion of goals is the starting point of your business that provides strategic vision and direction for the organization from its inception. Therefore, revise your statement when it no longer captures the essence of your business goals and

106

philosophies, loses relevance, or when it no longer inspires support from staff, customers, and other supporters.

In conclusion, create a statement that sparks enthusiasm. Find a way to set apart and clearly identify yourself, your organization, and products, and how it all differs from the rest of the world. Thereafter, with minimum effort from your customer, you need to fully and quickly communicate the benefits of your goods or services to others, and provide a sound reason for them to buy from you. Otherwise, they will shop with your competitor. You may not specifically say it, but the purpose of your mission is to create customers for life, even though you may not be in business that long. This is the best way to do it.

One way I have addressed this key business component is by combining my mission statement with an assurance or guarantee to my customers. I have named it "MY PLEDGE." It is a personal promise from me that I publish on brightly colored paper that clearly and openly contrasts with invoices and other paperwork associated with the transaction:

MY PLEDGE

Hello! You don't know me, but I would like to take a brief moment to explain my merchandising philosophy and promise to you, my customer. Although I am just a teenager, I was taught from early on that all a man really has to sell is his time and his reputation. My name and reputation in the community is far more important to me than the monetary gain on any sale.

I continually strive to advertise and sell products to you as represented. Your item was carefully packed and I hope it arrived safely, and that you are happy with your selection. However, I am not a professional merchant or expert. If there is any problem with your order, I would like to have the opportunity to make it right before you consider any other course of action. Hopefully this will never happen, but if anything is untoward with this order, I ask you to contact me before feedback, E-bay, or anyone else, and give me this chance. I promise to be honest, fair, and respond quickly to all customer inquiries, and I always participate in E-BAY FEEDBACK. I hope you do the same. Thank you for your business, trust, and confidence.

Austin Hoffman
guerillagaragesales.com

This heartfelt "oath" from me is enclosed in *every* package that I ship to my customers. The response from the buying public has been overwhelming, gratifying, and positive. Finally, writing down lofty goals like this is one thing. It is relatively easy to momentarily impress the reader with feel-good objectives. Like anything else with lasting value, however, once you say something, you promise it, and you must continually focus on your mission to actually *d o* what you say you believe, no matter what. As *Aristotle* once said: "We are what we repeatedly do…" The strange part is that it generally succeeds. Let me appeal to your sense of doing things my way.

XI

RETAIN GOVERNMENT RECORDS IN TRIPLICATE

In the autumn of 2002, when D.C. snipers John Muhammad, and his teenage accomplice, John Lee Malvo, began their murderous shooting rampage in the northeast beltway in and around Maryland, Virginia, and the nation's capitol, I briefly became involved with the FBI in the investigation of the sniper shootings. Even though I was in Texas and quite removed from this incident, like most of the country, I was caught up in the news and notoriety being generated by this horrific national tragedy. Almost every day it seemed like some innocent person was randomly being shot and killed near the nation's beltway. One night as I watched the evening news, I was intrigued when someone from the task force investigating these vicious crimes held up an assault rifle and indicated that it was most likely the type weapon being used in the shootings. Anyone who might have any information was encouraged to come forward, and a toll free telephone number to a national tip line was provided for the public to utilize for this purpose. The task force announced that no information would be considered too insignificant. For some reason I felt a little funny. Something registered in the back of my mind. I mulled it over for a while and then I went to my business records. After some 15 minutes of searching my paperwork, I was jolted by a revelation. Almost one month to the day before the first sniper shooting, I had sold an individual three brand new riflescopes for use by a gun exactly like the one being sought by the sniper task force. My sale had been to a man in Gaithersburg, Maryland—ACTUAL GROUND ZERO FOR THE SNIPER SHOOTINGS—and the clincher was his e-mail address. He went by the handle: *DELTADEATH*! I called the tip line and reported the details of this transaction. An operator said this was good information and

109

someone would get right back to me, however, no one called. Almost two weeks later I was in the shower getting ready for school. My mom banged on the door to my room and said that I had a telephone call. I asked who it was. She said it was the FBI.

"Sure!" I said, "no—really, who is it?"

"It's an agent with the FBI in Washington," my mother said. The agent identified himself and apologized for taking so long to get back to me. He said they had received over 75,000 calls on the tip line, they were working around the clock, and this was the earliest anyone could contact me. Basically, without divulging the nature and content of the investigation, I was able to provide all of the information the task force needed to follow up on this lead. The agent thanked me for my cooperation and said that he felt my lead was serious enough that a couple of agents were going to give this person a visit right away. I was able to perform this task quickly and completely because I had good records, my records were well organized, and double entry, which means that I had two ways to retrieve and review any sales transaction.

My fifteen minutes of fame and involvement with the FBI highlights the importance of good record keeping. Now, very few of us will ever have the good fortune of working with FBI agents in the solving of a major crime, but we all will be directly involved with another government agency—the Internal Revenue Service. If you do not know anything about income taxes remember one thing: you do not want to fall into the clutches of the IRS! The best way to avoid problems with your taxes and this governmental agency is to keep and maintain good business records for all purchases, expenses, income, gains, deductions, and every other financial detail directly associated with the operation of your business. Even though I was a teenager when I started, I learned that the government does not make any age distinction when it comes to taxes. Everyone is expected to know the law. Everyone is expected to comply with the tax code, or suffer the same penalty. There is no exception to this rule!

Secondly, most states have a state income tax system. Federal income tax information will most likely dovetail with your state's income tax requirements. Generally, most records you maintain for the IRS should, in most instances, be adequate for state income tax purposes. However, you also need to become familiar with your particular state's requirements in order to tailor your record keeping to easily and fully comply with the preparation and filing of your state return as well. Finally, you need to organize all of your business records, maintain them for years, and have a system for the retrieval of all vital business information. Information retrieval is necessary not only for tax purposes, but also to analyze your business and make decisions about future operations, including keeping up with your inventory, supplies, and other expenses.

The following is a simple system of record keeping that I developed for my business. I am by no means taking the position this is the best way, nor am I recommending anyone adopt my system verbatim for his own business. I do recommend that everyone should develop his own system. But, no matter what system you may utilize for your particular business, try to keep it simple, be certain you understand its operation, and have a speedy and accurate method to retrieve information and in-house intelligence.

The first thing I do when I sell an item is make *two* copies of the invoice provided by the site I am utilizing—like eBay. One invoice is for the buyer. I place the buyer's copy inside their shipping package. The other copy is for my records. When creating the copy for your records, be extremely thorough, precise, and consistent in your record keeping method. Remember, garbage in, garbage out—your records are only as good as the underlying information you keep and maintain. And, the information never gets any better. Always be certain and vigilant that the information contained on the pre-printed invoice contains all the vital information you might ever need for each transaction, including but not limited to: the date of the sale, the time, item number, name and complete address of the buyer, a brief item description, sales price of the item, a breakdown of commissions and fees charged, shipping information, including expenses, account numbers, payment information, etc. If all of the vital information is not contained on the invoice, add it by hand *immediately* and do not procrastinate, because this might be the only link you will ever have to the transaction.

Next, I save the transaction and load it into my computer database. There are many types of databases out there for you to use. No one is better than the other, but selection of a service depends on your preferences. My choice was *Microsoft Access*, only because I have *Microsoft Office* and they are part of a package. However, you can also use other database programs such as *Corel Paradox* or *FileMaker*. These databases are all wonderful, powerful, programs, which are easy to use. They all offer many capabilities, including managing your inventory, auctions, accounts, addresses, payments, records, and everything else involved in your business. Although it may take a while to get started, it is well worth your time. *There is no substitute for good record keeping!* For the computer illiterate, there is plenty of available information for utilizing database managers. Besides the help topics and tutorials within the database program itself, there are also many books and publications on the subject. After some research you can learn general database principles and should be able to build a custom database application to suit your own needs.

Following the sale and database entry, I place my invoice in my shipping pouch with the items to be shipped that day in my Hummer H-2. Most of the items shipped in my business are via the United States Postal Service. At the completion of each transaction, the Post Office provides each customer with a detailed receipt.

It contains the name and location of the facility where the items were shipped and other vital information about the postal facility. The receipt also contains the date and time of shipment with the hour and minute of the shipment noted at the top. Each item being shipped is contained on the receipt and is given a numerical listing, the type of delivery is noted along with the weight, destination zip code, cost per item, insurance, delivery confirmation, and other information, such as the total charges paid, and the manner of payment is provided. If I pay by credit card, I staple a copy of the credit card receipt to the main shipping receipt. *SAVE THIS RECEIPT!* This is a vital tax business record to memorialize what your business shipped and the costs associated with such transaction. Without it you cannot effectively deduct your expenses. In addition, you will not be able to establish to anyone's satisfaction that you actually shipped the item. You will frequently receive an e-mail from a buyer requesting the status of his shipment. And, if there is a lost or damage item in shipment, you will not be able to collect the insurance reimbursement without this paperwork.

After shipment I reconcile each sales invoice with the receipt from the shipper. I validate the number of items from each invoice to be certain that each item was actually shipped. Moreover, I verify and double-check the zip codes on the invoices to be sure they coincide with the items detailed on the receipt. Finally, I hand write the last name of each buyer being shipped on the back of the receipt, and I add the date and time of shipment to each of my invoices by writing it on the top of the invoice, and indicating it was shipped. You now have two different records to

UNITED STATES POSTAL SERVICE

```
***** WELCOME TO *****
    TYLER DOWNTOWN STA.
   TYLER,TEXAS 75702-7254
       02/28/05 07:58AM

Store  USPS         Trans    1
Wkstn  sys5004      Cashier  KR453Q
Cashier's Name      JIMMY
Stock Unit Id       CASH01
PO Phone Number     903-593-7525
USPS #              4822710710

 1. Media Mail                 1.84
    Destination:  77379
    Weight:       1 lb. 7.90 oz.
    Postage Type: PVI
    Total Cost:   1.84
    Base Rate:    1.84
 2. Media Mail                 1.42
    Destination:  85364
    Weight:       15.50 oz.
    Postage Type: PVI
    Total Cost:   1.42
    Base Rate:    1.42
 3. Media Mail                 1.42
    Destination:  37323
    Weight:       7.60 oz.
    Postage Type: PVI
    Total Cost:   1.42
    Base Rate:    1.42
 4. Media Mail                 1.42
    Destination:  11763
    Weight:       9.70 oz.
    Postage Type: PVI
    Total Cost:   1.42
    Base Rate:    1.42
 5. Media Mail                 1.42
    Destination:  01062
    Weight:       12.20 oz.
    Postage Type: PVI
    Total Cost:   1.42
    Base Rate:    1.42
 6. First Class                1.29
    Destination:  12603
    Weight:       4.40 oz.
    Postage Type: PVI
    Total Cost:   1.29
    Base Rate:    1.29
 7. First Class                1.29
    Destination:  37146
    Weight:       4.50 oz.
    Postage Type: PVI
    Total Cost:   1.29
    Base Rate:    1.29
 8. First Class                1.29
    Destination:  18337
    Weight:       4.40 oz.
    Postage Type: PVI
    Total Cost:   1.29
    Base Rate:    1.29
 9. Media Mail                 1.42
    Destination:  12983
    Weight:       9.10 oz.
    Postage Type: PVI
    Total Cost:   1.42
    Base Rate:    1.42

Subtotal                      12.81
Total                         12.81

VISA                          12.81
         <23-903021244-96>
VISA
ACCT. NUMBER       EXP     CLERK ID
XXXX XXXX XXXX 5757 01/07   01
AUTH 02887C  CREDIT TRANS # 259

ALL SALES FINAL ON STAMPS AND POSTAGE.
REFUNDS FOR GUARANTEED SERVICES ONLY.

Number of Items Sold: 9
```

Handwritten list:
1. Kuefler
2. Karcheunas
3. Moore
4. Pierre
5. Strack
6. Nicholetta
7. Scott
8. Bronstein
9. Eaby

refer to for each transaction. You have the sales invoice and the shipping receipt.

With all of this time spent on record keeping, it would be terrible tragedy if your computer cashed and the record was lost! Most business establishments maintain a computer backup system and so should you. A computer backup is as simple as saving your files on a floppy disk or compact disk (CD). As simple and inexpensive as this may be, you would be surprised how many people fail to utilize this important protective system. Either they are lazy and procrastinate, or they are so naïve as to believe that their computer is immune to all viruses, power outages, or any other calamity that may befall their hardware. I loathe admitting that for the longest time I failed to install a data backup. It only took one lightning storm and a fried motherboard to get my attention. Having a computer backup system is not an option, it is a necessity!

I maintain two depositories during the year for my business records. Depending on the nature of the search or information I am being provided about a particular transaction, I have two different places to search for each transaction. No one can keep perfect records, but if I make a mistake or omit information on one record, I usually find it is contained or correct on the other record. I maintain one box for sales invoices. I keep each sales invoice in chronological order by date in one box. I keep shipping receipts and all other expense business receipts in a second box. At the end of the year, after the preparation and filing of my federal income tax return, I place all of these records in a large container and store them in a safe, clean, dry place for at least seven years.

Another important record that is not peculiar to the garage sale business is the receipt, or proof of purchase, for items obtained at garage sales. Basically, this does not exist! The normal practice in the industry is that this is a cash business. It takes too much time to get a receipt, no one wants to fool with them, each sale is usually for a nominal amount, and the typical seller is not a businessperson, which means they do not utilize or even *have* receipts. Moreover, if you request a receipt, this will be a solid indication that you are a dealer or professional and the price of the sales item would likely escalate. Of course, purchase of "big ticket" items such as a Bradley Fighting Vehicle for the motor pool, furnishings for the barracks, appliances for the mess hall, electronics, and other large purchases for your hangar would probably generate a check or written receipt that can be utilized for your business records. Whenever possible, the safest practice is to get a receipt for these

GUERILLA GARAGE SALES

items and all other transactions. Most sales, however, do not involve a written memorandum of the transaction. How do you protect yourself and try to comply with the requirements of the applicable federal and state tax laws to deduct your cash expenses without written proof? I am not a lawyer or Certified Public Accountant. I will tell you what I do, but I am not recommending this method to you or implying in any way that it is legal in any jurisdiction, or in compliance with state or federal tax guidelines. In fact, my CPA informed me that it does not strictly comply, but it is better than nothing, which is more than most people do.

On the back of my itinerary I keep a running total of all purchases that I make each day attending garage sales. After I return home, I cut out the ads from the newspapers listing the garage sale addresses I outlined and attended. I make certain the ad includes the published date of the newspaper. I staple the ads to the back of my itinerary. On the front of the itinerary I list the total of all my purchases, and on the opposite side of the page I list the total of my mileage actually expended. Finally, depending upon the number of items that I may buy, I make a list of each purchase, and outline a detailed description so that anyone could identify my purchases at a later date, if necessary. I include the date of purchase, price paid, any identifying marks, the location of the purchase, and the condition of the item.

If you are ever challenged, this provenance will be some evidence of your expenditures, and if it is reasonable, hopefully it will be accepted, but I have been told that the IRS does not have to accept this or any other record.

Each day I maintain a computer spreadsheet detailing my income and expense portions of my business. There are numerous spreadsheet programs on the market. I do not feel that one spreadsheet program is superior to another. Find one with the features you need and operating components that you find most comfortable. Spreadsheets are ready made for detailing income and expenses because of their inherent calculating and accounting capabilities. No more writing on scratch paper or fumbling with your calculator. You have only to input basic data into your computer and the spreadsheet takes care of the rest, including all mathematical calculations. Each day you will know the bottom line and have a good idea how much you owe to Uncle Sam. Is this a good thing or bad?

Oh, in case you are wondering, my tip to the sniper hotline did not pan out. The gentleman I had implicated in the heart of the killing fields with the ominous sounding e-mail—was innocent. He was merely a retired member of the military, who, like the beltway victims, was in the wrong place at the wrong time. It turns out that *DeltaDeath* was a part of a slogan associated with his unit in his branch of prior military service that he adopted, in part, for his e-mail address. Imagine!

XII

UNCLE SAM NEEDS YOU

When I started my business five years ago, I could tell you the atomic number of magnesium, but I had no idea what form to use in filing my income tax return. Fortunately, there were many resources to access in fulfilling my federal tax responsibilities. It may be hard to believe, but the Internal Revenue Service remains one of the best providers of helpful, free taxpayer information.

As a new business owner, initially you need to decide if you will operate your business under some recognized legal entity apart from yourself, or simply in your own name. The top options are: sole proprietorship (see IRS Publication 334); partnerships (see IRS Publication 541); corporations (see IRS Publication 542); or Limited Liability Company (see IRS Publication 8832). You must have one of two forms of federally approved identification to file your taxpayer returns and other related documentation, i.e., a Social Security Number issued by the Social Security Administration (use application Form SS-5) by calling 1-800-772-1213, or access online at www.ssa.gov), *or* secure a federal identification number from the IRS. A federal identification number can be obtained online at www.irs.gov/business/small, by telephone at 1-800-829-4933, or by mailing or faxing an application Form SS-4. During the first calendar year of business operation you must adopt an accounting method (cash or accrual) to report income and expenses (see IRS Publication 334). Not all expenses are deductible as business expenses. How to deduct business start-up costs is contained in Chapter 9 of IRS Publication 535. Some business property such as furniture, buildings, machinery, and equipment cannot be deducted entirely in the year of purchase (see IRS Publication 946). If you do not rent or buy office space, it is possible to claim a deduction for a home office, but you must comply with

117

CASH HOFFMAN

the stringent requirements of rules enumerated in IRS Publication 587. If you use a car or truck in your business, you can deduct the cost of operating and maintaining it (see IRS Publication 463). If you have inventory that will not sell you may be taxed on it at the end of the year. Tax laws allow a deduction for cash or non-cash contributions to charitable organizations if you can itemize deductions on Schedule A of IRS Form 1040. Non-cash contributions are anything of value except cash. If you want to be certain that an organization is qualified by the IRS to receive tax-deductible donations, call the IRS Exempt Organization toll-free number at 1-877-829-5500 or visit the IRS website at www.irs.gov. Further information on how to deduct charitable contributions is available in IRS Publication 526 or by calling 1-800-829-3676. Every businessperson should keep reliable records to satisfy the established regulations of the IRS, the federal tax code, and the state tax laws where you reside. The rationale for good record keeping is obvious: to manage the progress of your business, prepare financial statements for lenders and other third parties, to be able to clearly identify income and expenses, and prepare your state and federal income tax returns. In addition to preparing your various tax returns, you must assemble, maintain and store all business related supporting documentation such as canceled checks, receipts, bank deposits, invoices, and other business records which support gross income figures and business deductions. These business records are easier to maintain and retrieve if the business affairs of the company are transacted in a separate bank account and not commingled with other business accounts or your personal account (see IRS Publication 583 with examples). You are required to keep all tax records for several years. The requisite time period differs based upon the type of return you file (see IRS Publication 583). There is more information about unresolved tax issues available from the IRS. A taxpayer may obtain additional information in several ways. Contact a Taxpayer Advocate at 1-877-777-4778, visit the website at www.irs.gov/advocate, or see IRS Publication 1546. There is a Small Business Tax Education Program readily accessible for small business owners and self-employed individuals to learn about business tax obligations. Call your local IRS office, or toll free 1-800-829-1040, to get answers to federal tax questions, or see IRS Publication 910. You can access the IRS website 24/7 at www.irs.gov for a host of other helpful information guides. You may order 100 of the top requested tax forms and instructions at 703-487-4608 or receive them by FAX at 703-368-9694. You can receive a list of publications offered by the IRS such as *Your Federal Income Tax and*

GUERILLA GARAGE SALES

Tax Guide for Small Business, by calling 1-800-829-3676. You can also order forms, instructions, and publications at this number and receive them at your HQ in approximately 10 days. Tax questions can be answered by landline at 1-800-829-4933. There is a recorded information line at 1-800-829-4477 covering over 140 timely federal income tax topics. There is a CD-ROM produced for small businesses by the IRS, which is a handy guide for any small business owner or any taxpayer about to start a business. The CD is interactive and contains all the business tax forms, instructions, and other publications most small business operators normally need to conduct their business in compliance with the tax laws. Call 1-800-829-3676 or visit online at www.irs.gov/smallbiz. If you may need any other type of business assistance, the Small Business Administration (SBA) provides financial aid, training programs, and other logistical support to current and prospective small business owners. You can access the SBA website at www.sba.gov or call 1-800-827-5722. Numerous federal agencies publish instructional materials for small businesses. You can locate information and pamphlets for assistance at www.access.gpo.gov, or call 1-800-866-1800. You may also write to:

Superintendent of Documents
P. O. Box 371954
Pittsburgh, PA 15250-7954

If you choose to prepare and file your own income tax return, there are several commercial computer programs on the market that are designed specifically for this purpose, including H & R Block Financial's *"Tax Cut,"* Intuit's *"Turbo Tax"* and *"MacInTax."* There are several helpful links to further assist you in the preparation of your taxes:

www.taxprophet.com
www.aicpa.org
www.ey.com

In conclusion, if the IRS ever comes knocking on your door, you can never have too many business records. There's peace of mind in taking care of Uncle Sam and doing your homework, but the truth is no one is truly prepared. Onward and upward.

XIII

PHOTO RECONNAISSANCE

You don't have to be a photographer to be a prolific online seller, but it would not hurt. Nowhere is this truer than on eBay. In fact, having a picture of your item will increase the likelihood of selling it by over 80%! Moreover, 90% of eBay listings include pictures, so you really have no choice if you want to compete on the web. You simply cannot operate in this marketplace without a camera. The camera of choice for the Internet photographer, whether professional or amateur, is a digital camera. For some reason the word "digital" scares a lot of people, but the basic mechanics involved in taking pictures with a digital camera are the same as a conventional camera—follow a few simple rules in preparation, then point and shoot! There is really nothing to fear. After all, a digital camera is *a camera*, not a defibrillator. If you have ever taken pictures with any type of film camera, and the pictures were developed, you can use a digital camera. There are no training prerequisites or any special technique *per se* that distinguish digital from film photography. The main parts of a digital camera are almost identical to its counterpart. Digital cameras have the same basic features that film models possess, including: zoom lens, built-in flash, viewfinder, auto focus, a battery, a shutter—and the push of a button takes the picture. There is no mystery to it. The most notable difference between digital and film hardware is that digital cameras do not use film, they operate with a computer chip known as a charged coupling device (CCD), similar to those contained in video cameras. The CCD is a grid of miniature light-sensitive diodes that convert photons (light) into electrical impulses. Bright light produces a stronger electrical impulse than dimmer photons. Once the image you capture in the camera lens is reduced to electrical impulses, the computer chip converts the impulses into millions of tiny dots that are stored dot by dot in the camera's mini-computer storage memory. Each dot is called a *pixel*, which is an acronym for *"picture elements."* The more pixels there are in an image, the higher the resolution, and the better the quality of the photograph. Two numbers specifying width and height identify the resolution of a digital picture. For example, the following picture coordinates *1024 x 768*, denote dots per square inch (dpi). The degree of sharpness of the picture can also be referred to as "bits per pixel." When the computer chip reads each pixel, the internal software also assigns a color to it, called a *tonal value*. Thus, when the picture is recalled from the camera's memory, it exactly reproduces and displays the original image on a viewing screen. Once the photons are converted to electricity, the CCD converts the electricity to pixels, and pixel dots are stored on the camera's memory hard drive, an image is said to be *"digitized."* Digital cameras store pictures as computer files. The image stays in the camera hard drive, is available for immediate use, and can be manipulated within the computer, or transmitted over external computer networks indefinitely. Unlike film negatives, digital images will not degrade over time if properly stored.

There is another important digital vs. film difference. The object you photograph is instantly displayed on a screen on the back of the camera for your review before and after the shot. This is an invaluable aid in producing sales ads because you can instantly review a fully developed picture without waiting. If you have a camera powered by rechargeable batteries, taking pictures is virtually free since there is no cost in film or developing. As soon as you snap the shutter, the image is instantly ready to view on your camera or computer monitor. Take as many pictures as you want, or your camera's memory will hold. If you want to take additional pictures over the limit, you can replace the memory "card" in the camera or download pictures into your computer, to free up camera memory. It is also easy to delete shots in the camera you do not like, on the spot, and replace them with new ones, keeping only those you prefer. No one can ruin your shots with flawed film processing, because there is nothing to develop or do after you push the shutter button. Once you take a picture, it is stored in the camera forever until you decide what you want to do with it. The digital camera never runs out of "film." Its memory chip can be re-deployed an unlimited number of times as long as you have battery power.

Before purchasing an expensive camera, it is crucial to know how you will deploy it in the field. For purposes of this discussion I will assume that you intend to primarily use your camera on the Internet. Buy a camera that does most of the work for you because on the Net, simple is best. Furthermore, buy a camera for close-up photography indoors, because most pictures will be taken in close quarters—within two feet or less. For Internet consumption, you can adequately photograph most objects with a low-resolution digital camera. Besides cost, you also may want a low-resolution system because it takes less time to download on the Net. However, when compared to film cameras, most digital cameras are notably lower in resolution anyway. The good news is that you do not necessarily have to purchase an extremely expensive or complex photographic system with high-resolution capabilities. If you follow a few simple rules, you can produce pictures that will contain enough detail to readily assist you in selling your products on eBay and most other sites. Having the right camera to the photographer is like Tiger Woods teeing off with the correct golf club! The problem is Tiger has a bag full of clubs to tackle any shot, and you have to choose one camera for every shot. When making a decision on which digital camera to buy, do not base your determination on price alone, you also need to consider resolution. Did you ever hear the old saying: *A picture is worth a million pixels*? Probably not, but just as important as price, a deciding factor in your purchase should be the *megapixel* capacity. Digital cameras express resolution in "megapixels" (one million pixels). The greater the pixel output of your digital camera, the higher the resolution, and the sharper the images it will generate. I personally use a 3-megapixel digital camera and recommend it to everyone interested in all around selling on eBay and most other sites. Before you make a decision, buy a camera with the highest resolution and features you want, and consider the following:

☠   1-Megapixel Digital Cameras—Ideal for basic usage, such as e-mailing photos, posting photos on the Web, and printing small, everyday shots.

☠   2-Megapixel Digital Cameras—Perfect for general usage, including e-mailing photos, posting photos on the Web, and printing everyday shots.

GUERILLA GARAGE SALES

☠   3-Megapixel Digital Cameras—Suitable for average photographers and high-quality general use. Good for both everyday and special occasions.

☠   4+ Megapixel Digital Cameras—owned by avid photographers who want near-35mm (film) quality results.

Before investing in a digital photographic system, there are two initial accessory decisions you will have to resolve—memory and batteries. Most stock digital cameras have the capacity to hold about 25 pictures, and are usually sold and designed with a low RAM capability. Often the accompanying literature provides information on how many pictures you can take at the highest quality setting. Just like computers, the more RAM you have, the more pictures you can take without having to download or replace memory. There are various types of interchangeable memory devices you can utilize to enlarge and enhance the picture capacity of your camera. Depending on the quality and quantify of picture taking you elect when selecting hardware, make sure your camera has more than enough RAM. When it comes to batteries, use the heavy-duty lithium kind. Digital cameras expend a lot of power and disposable batteries do not last very long. If your batteries are exhausted the camera cannot operate, and weak batteries may cause a number of technical problems in the operation of the digital camera. Rechargeable batteries are better, but if you can afford it, I recommend a rechargeable battery pack or charging cradle for maximum effectiveness and battery longevity. Always keep spare batteries on hand, even the rechargeable ones.

Besides deciding what digital camera to buy, you also have to decide where to buy it. Shop for your equipment at a local store where the staff is knowledgeable and can demonstrate and explain the various features and functions of your camera and its accessories before your purchase. Finally, if you shop locally, you will have someone to confer with from time to time after the sale, also to be accountable for warranty work if you have problems with your camera.

The basic rules and techniques of film photography are just as applicable to digital, with a few unique differences. Whether you are an amateur or more advanced in your photographic skills, there are a few things you need to master in order to take good online digital pictures:

⊕ Create your own photo workshop: It does not have to be very fancy. Choose a convenient place close to natural light. If the designated area does not have a light, plain background, tape poster board or drape a large cloth to soften the shooting area. I use a kitchen counter top. The counters are an off white color and located near an entire wall of floor to ceiling windows. There is also large skylight overhead. Several electrical outlets flank the wall nearby and this facilitates placement of additional spot lighting whenever necessary. Because the counter area is large, often I can just move the shot or my equipment to avoid shadows or glare. It is very easy to set up my equipment and tear down. This has been an ideal photographic workspace, except at suppertime.

⊕ Get it right with light: There are several elements in creating a good shot, but lighting is critical. Lighting is more difficult with digital cameras. If you are a beginner, natural light is the easiest to manage. Practice with it first. Use your flash sparingly because a flash can change the tone of the picture and waste your battery power. Avoid direct light that will wash out the image or cause a glare to appear. If you do not flood your shot with too much light, most cameras come with enhancing software that will allow you to brighten the image and manipulate it in other ways inside your computer. I was told that artificial, halogen or florescent lights could adversely affect your picture quality because they constantly flicker, but I have not experienced any adverse effects.

⊕ Get up close to your shot: You are trying to sell your product, not the photograph. Do not try to worry about composition, fancy camera angles, or other stylistic approaches in the name of art. Get in as close with your lens as you possibly can to show all the detail of the object you are selling. The buyer wants to verify condition, so provide the clearest possible picture of your item, if you want to make the sale.

⊕ You do not necessarily have to include the entire item in your shot. If you are concerned about displaying the item in its entirety, fill the frame and take a second shot for more detail. It is all right to cut off edges and parts of the shot in order to show up-close detail.

✦ When photographing, fill the frame as much as possible to make your photo *online ready*. After you transfer your camera files to your computer, there are enhancing software programs that allow you to adjust the size and brightness and other features of your picture. Do not become dependent or overemphasize the intended purpose of picture editing software. That is backwards. I believe the better approach is to maximize your shot and only utilize the enhancement features as they were intended. Once you take your pictures, you need to edit them. Often, a CD-ROM with picture software for transferring and editing digital pictures is included with your camera system purchase. If you do not receive picture software, or just want to experiment with different types and features, I recommend Adobe Photoshop. You can download at no charge by visiting their website at www.adobe.com. This freeware manipulates all the essentials, including cropping, rotating, contrasting, and changing the light to touch up, edit, and enhance your digital pictures. If you need more enhancement and other special features, you can upgrade to Adobe Elements Professional and Adobe 3.0. These upgrades are normally not necessary for most digital images you will employ in your business. However, if you list valuable art, collectibles, paintings, motor vehicles or other large objects, this type of enhancing software purchase would be a worthwhile investment.

⊕ Use a tripod: The human body is unable to hold a camera perfectly still and avoid blurred shots. This fact of life is aggravated by an inherent mechanical time delay in taking digital pictures. From the time you push the shutter it takes over a second for the camera to take the photo. A lot can happen even during that short period of time. Even slight movement can blur the picture. The delay is caused by the time it takes the auto-focus to set up. On some cameras you can reduce this time lag by pressing the button halfway down until you hear the auto focusing function activating. Then when you further press and complete the shutter action, there should be a much shorter delay. The best pictures are taken with steady cameras. Consequently invest in a tripod. A good tripod offers you enough versatility so that you can pan, tilt, and adjust the height of your camera to take any picture you want, with a minimum of effort or damage to your equipment. Besides a tripod, for taller shots in my kitchen, I sometimes use a butcher block on wheels to steady my camera. Also, I have collected some plastic steps that were used in conjunction with exercise videos. I use these to elevate my camera tripod for certain shots. Depending on the type of inventory you have for sale, you may want to consider a miniature, tabletop tripod. Whenever I am shooting smaller items, I frequently use one that has six-inch adjustable legs. If you find a way to steady it, you can also use the miniature tripod for "taller" shots.

⊕ Avoid conspicuous backgrounds: Once again, you are selling a product. You need to showcase that product and nothing else. Fill the frame with your item. Do not display it with other products or things if they are not being sold together. Do not interpose anything in the frame that takes attention away from your item, such as your cat, household furniture, clutter, or other distracting backgrounds. When you become more experienced there are ways to add depth and color to your shot by coordinating with colorful backgrounds and other objects, but do not try this right away.

⊕ Take lots of pictures: The beauty of digital is that there is virtually little, if any cost to produce your images. There is very little downside. Take as many photos as you want to capture that special shot when everything comes together. You learn by experience and regular practice. After a while you will develop your own style and pinpoint your likes and dislikes. Ultimately, your pictures will improve and your sales will skyrocket. Time is your best friend.

⊕   Plan your shot: Be patient. You can take a hundred shots with little cost, but that takes time. Do not waste time for no reason. Set up for the best use of available light. Try to anticipate shadows and glare. Plan how you want to photograph your item in the best light possible and show all of its attributes. If you get all of the details right the first time you will not have to re-shoot.

⊕   Utilize Angles: Every image does not have to be on the horizontal or vertical plane. For interest, occasionally use an angle or off-center shot to highlight your subject. Take a bold approach to your photography.

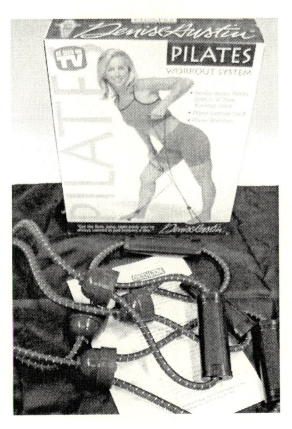

⟡ Use close-ups: To illuminate or concentrate on important details of your subject, use close-ups. The buyer will appreciate the view and open his pocketbook.

⟡ Become more professional: No matter what your level of experience, you can always improve. Check out competitor listings on eBay and other sites. Analyze what others are doing well and imitate their best techniques. Make them your own and improve upon them. Focus on areas of photography where you want to excel. Subscribe to professional magazines and periodicals that interest you. Go to your public library, or study online. Ask questions; you can learn a lot. There is a new online digital-only photography source—*photopheed.com*—a search engine which offers daily syndicated original news and content feeds from across the Internet, as well as blogs, forums, and reviews that are all continuously updated and archived for use by amateur and professional digital photographers.

Another method in adding photos to your listings is with a film camera and scanner. If you already own a good camera and are not looking to make a big investment in photography, consider this approach. Although cheaper than digital cameras, the quality of images is sometimes not as good. If you are interested in purchasing a scanner to take your pictures, here is a description of each type:

Flatbed Scanners: As the name implies, these scanners have a flat surface that holds the item you wish to scan. Flatbed scanners are flexible and able to hold bulky sources such as books and magazines (as long as they fit on the scan surface). However, since they are flat, they take up more desk space.

Sheetfed Scanners: These scanners automatically feed the pages through, pulling them over a fixed scanning device. While they are limited to single-page sources such as photos and loose-leaf papers, they are much more compact than flatbed scanners, require less space on your desk, and can be moved about more easily to satisfy portable scanning needs.

Film Scanners: Scanners in this category are dedicated to 35mm negatives and slides. Unlike flatbed and sheetfed scanners (which cast light up and then read the reflection, which can cause problems with transparent sources like film, where nothing is reflected), film scanners are specially designed to use a backlight that projects light through the film so it can be read by the scanner. The dedication pays off, since digital images scanned from film are more detailed and color-rich.

The third way to add photos to your eBay listings is through a film-to-digital image service. This option is more convenient than scanners and is perfect for those who cannot spend that much time on listings. With this option, you can take a picture of the item you are selling with a traditional film camera, take it to a photo center, (Wal-Mart, Kinko's, Walgreen's, etc.) and have them develop it for you. Then you can access the pictures online, and upload them into your eBay listings. However, there is one disadvantage to this service. The average cost for the photo center to submit the pictures online adds an extra $2.00 to the film development cost. After a while, this can really add up! In my opinion it may be wise to invest in the digital camera, which will eventually end up paying for itself in the long term. Look closely. See the beauty of flowers in a junkyard.

XIV

LOGISTICAL SUPPORT

We have spent considerable time covering acquisition of inventory, cleaning and prepping merchandise, and vending on the Internet. Now we need to concentrate on the best way to pack and ship to your customers. The ultimate goal of every professional business establishment is a streamlined process for creating, managing, distributing, and delivering its products. In the world of *dots and coms*, shipping your products is an essential part of your overall business plan. The American market system has gone from a producer dominated system to a distribution dominated system. To compete today, you must put a professional game plan in play to service the shipping needs of your buyer, fulfill your overall marketing strategy, and make a profit. There are three shipping criteria you must address to satisfy your customers: pack securely and economically; deliver in a timely manner; and adopt a solid business philosophy to fulfill all current and prospective customer shipping requirements.

Initially, I want to take care of some housekeeping. In the past five years I have shipped some 8,500 objects of various sizes, shapes, and weight. I have sold diminutive items as small as a postage stamp. I have handled the transfer of a MGB convertible automobile, heavy machinery, jewelry, and a host of other effects in between. The bulk of my experience is based on shipping books, videos, games, DVD's and CD's, but I believe my limited shipping expertise will provide a useful starting point for you to reference when implementing your specific e-commerce shipping needs. From the outset, this discourse is published as *a guide, only* for newcomers to deal with most belongings and common everyday possessions found in most traditional households throughout the country. My packing and shipping techniques are not the "gospel" and should not be viewed by the reader as the only way to get the job done. No one should blindly adopt any suggestion in this book *carte blanche* to fill any shipping order they may encounter in their business. Although not necessarily unique, these methods have served me well. I suggest that you consider them to be the minimum standard for your general business shipping needs. Furthermore, you should *not utilize* these minimum standards if you intend to pack and ship extremely valuable or rare articles, antiques, or museum quality artifacts, because I have had no experience with such items. It is my understanding expensive crates and custom designed rigidly constructed cartons are employed in these instances, as well as the utilization of special carriers and shippers who are uniquely qualified to transport and deliver such items. Regardless of what you may face in your business practice, if in doubt, always solicit expert advice before you undertake any shipping task.

SHIP TIMELY

Like good service, timely product delivery does not simply happen. It has to be an integral part of your business plan. Timing is essential in business shipping, and you have to deliver economically, on time, every time. Although I do not advertise the fact, I ship within 24 hours of each order, six days a week. Shipping delays are at the top of the list of consumer complaints according to the Better Business Bureau. Furthermore, constant option evaluation and logistics have to be practiced, to keep costs down and customers happy. Besides getting the goods to the customer on time, as a business owner you have a responsibility to keep customers informed about the status of their orders, otherwise they become anxious, distrustful, and difficult. Whenever economically feasible, secure tracking numbers to trace the progress of your orders. Do not try to make a profit on shipping. Just cover your hard shipping costs and a small handling fee to offset some of your time and overhead. Hardly anything will irk a customer more than abnormally high shipping charges. Make a profit on your product inventory or find another product line because you *will lose* customers when you overcharge on shipping. Furthermore, each time you sell on eBay you are entering into a legally binding cartage contract—either a shipping contract or a delivery contract. You need to know the difference. If the contract is for *delivery*, you are responsible for getting the item to the purchaser and bear the risk of loss for damage occurring to goods after the sale has been completed but before delivery has been accomplished. In the normal course of business the seller chooses the shipping method, manner, and carrier. If something goes wrong, the carrier is the seller's agent and he will have to indemnify the buyer. On the other hand, a *shipping contract* immediately transfers ownership of the goods to the buyer once they are delivered to the carrier. In this instance, the carrier becomes the buyer's agent and the buyer's problem. Most e-commerce sites like eBay require a seller to meet certain prerequisites before they are able to shift shipping liability and risk of loss to a buyer.

PACKING

When the tread meets the road, good packaging is the most important part of a successful logistical support and shipping regimen. Getting your products into your customer's hands is complicated, and there is not a single solution. It is a disquieting statistic, but every parcel is subjected to various forms of trauma, vibration, and other external forces during shipment. Sometimes *en route* it may face onslaught from extreme temperatures and moisture. Therefore, it is crucial to pack the contents of each order correctly. Some of the finer points of tactical logistical support remain constant. According to general orders of intermediate planning, there are two major prongs of attack in preparing a package for transport.

First you need to select the proper box, mailing tube, or other solid enclosure to protect your item during shipment. In a nutshell, this means that you pack from the outside in, not the reverse. Initially, choose the main shipping container, which is usually a corrugated cardboard box. Operational necessity dictates that the container must be the optimal size. This means that you always allow sufficient room for the contents to be shipped in tandem with packing material, invoices, applicable dispatches, and nothing more, to minimize expense. Moreover, the characteristics of the contents to be shipped will ordain the tactical method, outer, and inner packing components to be employed in each instance. Small, less damage-prone items can generally be shipped in lighter, corrugated, cardboard boxes, with a minimum of padding or other protection. Hefty, oversize, or fragile items require more attention. They usually demand larger, more rigid boxes and additional padding and space to protect the contents, to assure they arrive unscathed. When shipping the latter, the outer packaging should be: sturdy and large enough so that the contents do not touch each other or the container sides directly, sufficiently configured to avoid content migration inside the cargo container, and strongly sealed at all key stress points, to maintain

GUERILLA GARAGE SALES

overall stability. In these latter instances you may want to avoid the use of some recycled boxes if they are not stable, sufficiently secure, or free from damage. One must be aware that the stability of a box is compromised the more it is reused. Before you reuse a container, always check for tears, perforations, and other forms of damage that affect stability. When in doubt discard the container. Additionally, you need to remove old seals and replace them to insure the used container will remain intact during transport. When you recycle a container always remove or block out any pre-existing writing, labels, or identifying/shipping marks on the box. If this is not done it could complicate or delay arrival of your shipment.

Secondly, the protective qualities of the outer packaging will always be ineffectual to protect your merchandise, if not coordinated and reinforced with good inner packaging techniques. The importance of good padding and adequate content restraint on the inside of the package cannot be overemphasized. A superior exterior container can never compensate for the lack of good inner packaging and vice versa. There are usually two steps to pad and secure the item within the package. Initially, wrap and tape each item separately in clean white Kraft wrapping paper, (butcher paper) or cover completely with a clear plastic water-resistant sheathing, like the garment bags you get from the dry cleaners. The purpose of this wrap is to protect the item from dirt and other contaminants, and help stabilize its location and shifting inside the container. Always wrap and tape each item before placing inside the box. You need to be aware there is a school of thought that shies away from, using of any type of plastic wrap for this purpose. Theoretically, if your item is sealed airtight in plastic or bubble wrap, an abrupt temperature drop could cause condensation to form inside the package and damage the item. (If you have a very valuable item, or are concerned about this possibility, use paper wrapping). Then, depending on the shape of the object, you need to further protect and secure each item by taping with stiff cardboard protectors, or encasing with solid blocks of plastic foam material, made from polystyrene that you usually find in consumer electronics boxes. This material is also available commercially in sheets of various thickness or blocks that can be easily fashioned to cradle and protect your cargo. The foam material should be securely taped to the object as well.

As you load into the shipping container, you need to further pad and cushion the wrapped object to protect it from external forces and minimize

133

shifting damage. You can do this by lining the box with a layer of foam sheeting, or placing on a bed of Styrofoam packing "peanuts" and then plug the gaps completely with more peanuts, until filled to the brim, or you can envelop the bundle snugly with bubble wrap. With the advent of increased security and personal shredding devices, some people occasionally use shredded paper for filler, in order to recycle and save on cost. Personally, I never use paper as filler. I do not believe it protects and maintains it shape as well as peanuts and bubble wrap, which also absorb shock better. Further, paper is considerably heavier and will result in higher shipping prices. Finish the operation by sealing the box. Use a strong sealing material that is adequate for the job, such as a heavy-duty gauge plastic shipping tape at least 1 7/8 inches in width. You can use a lighter duty gauge for smaller, less bulky packages. You can also use commercial gummed tape with the reinforcing fibers, however, never use masking tape, Scotch tape, insulation tape or other non-tear resistant products to seal your packages, because they are not strong enough to remain adhered to the package during shipment. Moreover, when sealing the package, tightly extend the tape completely around the box until it overlaps the beginning portion of the tape and then seal over the underlying tape after passing about three inches past the beginning seam. If you utilize this technique on each run of your tape, it provides overall sealing strength, making it more difficult for the tape to be loosened. On extremely large or heavy boxes you may want to further secure the container with plastic bands or twine.

MAILING TUBES

Some pictures, photographs, posters and paper products can be shipped in a cardboard mailing tube whenever it is not possible or practical to ship flat. Most often it is better to ship such items flat. Depending on the size of your item to be shipped, begin with a *very clean* wooden dowel pin one-quarter inch in diameter or smaller. On an *extremely clean surface*, using the dowel pin, beginning on one end of the item to be shipped, gently, but tightly roll it into the shape of a small compact tube, with the media side rolled inward. When finished rolling, hold the rolled item firmly in your hand to keep it from expanding. Carefully slide out the dowel pin so you do not scratch the product. Next, to safeguard your item during shipment while firmly grasping it to keep it from expanding, completely enclose the rolled item in a protective layer of paper or clear plastic. Then, cover with a layer of cushioning material, to further protect it during shipment. Be certain to wrap each layer firmly around your item while holding securely in your hand. Upon completion of the last layer, loosely tie off with rubber bands, string, or tape to keep the bundle from unrolling. I usually put a band at each end and in the middle of the item. *Note*: the tie restraints should only be tight enough to keep the item from unraveling. Do not band so taut as to make any indentations, or alter the round shape of the item. Then take an oversized mailing tube and insert the packaged material inside. To avoid damage, the completed package should be wrapped in such a way it can easily be removed from the tube without pulling on the object itself or pressing against the sides of the container. The shipping tube should also be large enough in diameter to accommodate the inserted material easily without forcing it into the tube. Further, when the item is centered equidistant in the tube, there should be at least two inches of empty space at each end of the mailer. Loosely pack the ends of the container with a soft "fill" material, and seal with an end cap. Finally, for further protection, seal the end cap with shipping tape to keep it from opening during transport. Finish with shipping and address labels. It is acceptable to reuse mailing tubes, but only if they remain stable and undamaged. If bends, perforations, or loose seams appear anywhere on the mailer, do not use it.

SHIPPING BOOKS

This section will outline general rules for packing books.

Most flat items and books are packed in almost identical fashion and configured in much the same way as many other shipping items. Begin with the first wrap—a clean paper or plastic material, as previously mentioned above, followed by a complete taping. More expensive volumes should be individually wrapped, whereas more moderately priced books can be wrapped together as a unit, if they are the same size. When books are wrapped together, it is always recommended that the exposed ends of the stack should have the back cover of each respective book facing outward, not the front cover. Also, you should position the least valuable books on the top and bottom of the stack. The rationale for this is the least valuable cover of the two most inexpensive books will most likely bear the brunt of any damage. Before wrapping, each volume in the stack should be staggered with the spine facing in one direction, then the next book's spine facing in the opposition direction, and so on.

When you finish stacking all of the books, (including first wrap of paper or plastic) tightly tape with the appropriate packing tape around the center, across the middle, and the outer edge of the stack. Run the tape in a continuous band until the stack is secure and the books are immovable inside their protective covering. The second wrapper should be a padding material like bubble wrap or corrugated plastic wrap that encloses and protects the entire book or book stack. If you have a large stack or heavy books, use this same method but break up the stack into several smaller stacks. I have personally never shipped more than twenty pounds of books in one cardboard container. There are several ways an individual book, or several small books can be wrapped a third time for even more protection. Depending on the size of the books or stack of books, the bundle can be placed in a smaller form-fitted cardboard box and sealed, before placement in the ultimate shipping container. Another way is to fashion cardboard end pieces and tape them to the books to protect the edges. Place a piece of cardboard on the front cover and a second piece on the back cover. The pieces should be fashioned from heavy cardboard and form-fitted so that the cardboard fully and equally overlaps each edge of the book covers by at least one-half inch all around each cover of the book, or several small bound books. Tape front and back cardboard book covers together for a secure hold while maintaining the half-inch protective overlap around the entire perimeter of the book(s). The individual book or stack of books can then be packaged in the shipping container or heavy-duty mailing envelope for final delivery. Another type of wrap may be utilized if you have a bundle with a thickness and size of not more than several standard newsstand magazines. Insert the wrapped book(s) in a recycled express-mail/overnight delivery envelope/mailer constructed of light duty cardboard. Seal the mailer and place in a thin box or a heavy-duty manila envelope for shipment. VCR tapes, CD's DVD's, and video games can be packaged and shipped like books, or wrapped and inserted into padded mailers. When using padded mailers be certain they are large enough to protect your item. Add additional padding, if necessary. Close the mailer and tape completely shut. Tape off each corner of the mailer to maintain a strong seal, address, attach appropriate labels, and ship.

SHIPPING CHARGES

Buyers on the Internet are wary of shipping cost scams. Most consumers are extremely hesitant to bid on items when the shipping costs are not fully disclosed, or calculable within the confines of the ad prior to the sale. Internet veterans are fully aware the successful bidder, by acquiescence, has agreed to honor all the terms of the Seller's offer. Oftentimes not all of the details are known when the gavel is bought down. This is an open-ended transaction and one can readily be at the mercy of the seller once the bidding has ended. If you have agreed to pay *the shipping costs*, but the amount is not fully enumerated in the ad, or furnished to you in advance, you have to pay *whatever the seller declares*! I am not an attorney, but I know that there are limits, and this is the basic problem. Some enterprising sellers have an interactive program contained in their online ad that is programmed to permit a buyer to immediately compute potential shipping costs to its location, by typing in a zip code before bidding. Others list fixed shipping costs in the body of their ad, so the buyer will be informed of this obligation, before actually committing by bid. The problem with fixed costs from the Seller's standpoint is obvious. Unless you carefully account for every transport possibility, you can lose money. You are committed to a fixed amount. Some sellers ask potential buyers to e-mail their zip codes prior to the sale and they will calculate shipping for them. This is ineffectual at times because e-mail communication is limited, particularly toward the end of the auction. I use a combination of methods. I list a fixed shipping amount in my sales ads, but before publishing it in black and white, I do a couple things. First I fully pre-pack the item, but I do not seal the package. To be safe, I occasionally drop in a little extra weight to allow for error. Then, I weigh the package on my digital scale, and based on my experience, I decide what carrier would be best suited to deliver the item. The final decision is a little tricky. In advance, I select the ideal location that represents the median terminal shipping point from my location. After some trial and error, Las Vegas was determined to be the ideal location for me. Consequently, whenever I quote a fixed price in my ad, I calculate the cost of delivery of the item to Las Vegas and post that amount on my site in advance. (I also include a small handling fee to offset my shipping costs). Even by quoting this exact price, I usually receive enough for my costs and expenses, and the buyer is satisfied. I occasionally have to cover additional shipping costs because of the buyer's location but my method works most of the time and it averages out over the year. Whenever posting fixed prices, be careful to limit the delivery area. For example, you may wish to declare *delivery in the continental United States only*, because even shipments to Hawaii and Alaska or other U.S. territories can impose an increased cost (except for Media Mail). Of course, posting this disclaimer does not keep you from ultimately shipping your advertised area if a buyer prevails upon you during the bidding process. Of course, selling abroad is always a possibility. There is strong, steady demand for American products around the globe. I have sold merchandise in many countries and provinces worldwide. Problems I have encountered have tempered me. I do not flatly take the position not to sell outside of this country. I wait for foreign nationals to contact me during bidding and ask if I would consider shipping a particular item to them. Some times I do. I pre-pack and take the item to the Post Office for an estimate and relay it to the buyer. (After the sale I go back to the same clerk to ship in the event the price is different on the final shipping). The problem with foreign transactions is the shipping costs. In my personal experience, the shipping expenses are often as much or more than the item price. You can ship overseas by air, or economy (which is usually a slow boat). Airmail delivery is around four to seven days. Economy is four to six weeks. There is no media mail postage break available in foreign countries unless the recipient is active U.S. military. Global Priority Mail sponsored by the United States Postal Service offers two flat rate envelopes for shipping abroad at a fixed rate. The large envelope is 9 ½ inches by 12 ½ inches in size and dispatches for $9.50. The smaller envelope is 10 inches by 6 inches and costs $5.25. If the shipping contents do not exceed four pounds and can be inserted in one of these envelope without additional packing or taping they will be accepted for mailing. This method is not approved for delivery to every country so check with the Post Office in advance.

Even though I may tell a prospective buyer about the cost up front, there are still occasional problems. Perhaps buyer's remorse sets in. When I ship economy, they often e-mail me and ask about their order even though it has not been long enough for delivery. Finally, after delivery, even though everything went as planned, they are unhappy. They cannot find fault with shipping, because costs were provided in advance. Naturally then, the focus is on the item itself. They will tell you they are disappointed with the quality or condition, or some other imagined problem with your merchandise. Another problem with foreign sales equally problematic is when you make a mistake. If you leave something out of an order, or have to compensate for an error on your part, the return shipping is a deal killer. Foreign shipments require completion and inclusion of a customs form with each package. Depending of the size and weight of the object, you must become familiar with two separate forms if you use the Post Office. These are some of the reasons I try to concentrate my commercial activity to the lower forty-eight!

Another area of concern to the average customer is "combined shipping" discounts. This occurs whenever a customer is the winning bidder simultaneously on two or more items belonging to one seller. In my opinion, working with buyers in this respect, is a good marketing opportunity to advertise and promote within a seller's web site sales listings. It is a win-win arrangement. Customers welcome it because it is convenient and saves them money on shipping costs. The net result is the Seller makes one delivery of multiple sales items to a single address. At the end of the day, both the seller and buyer save money. The buyer gets a reduced price for one delivery instead of paying the *"combined shipping"* costs of each individual item. The seller initially concedes some shipping revenue, but realizes a profit on multiple item sales, and saves money on multiple packaging costs by combining into one shipment. Although the savings to the Seller may be negligible when focusing on individual transactions, however, the concept encourages multiple sales, and that can add profits to the Seller's bottom line long term. Some sellers advertise *free shipping*. They use shipping expenses as a loss leader. This is usually a marketing strategy to attract buyers. Ultimately they have to increase the costs of their goods to make a profit—because nothing is *free*.

PACKAGE MARKING

To further protect your cargo, save time, and give your final product a professional appearance, use appropriate identifying stickers and labels. I usually post a sticker on at least four sides of any package requiring special shipping notices for the carrier to observe. As an additional time saver and operational necessity, you should produce or purchase a professional return address label to tag each shipment. Besides your pertinent information, I think the label should include your e-mail address in order for the purchaser to contact you for any reason. I routinely affix shipping condition labels to packages like *FRAGILE, DO NOT BEND* and *PROTECT FROM HEAT*. Depending on your particular shipping requirements, you may use these or many others available commercially. And, if you do not have a particular label available, you can create one with your computer and color printer.

CARRIERS

There are numerous commercial shipping carriers available for your worldwide use. I mainly use Federal Express and the United States Postal Service in my business. When doing business with the Post Office, priority mailing supplies are free. I ship USPS almost exclusively internationally. If you purchase an electronic scale, it will have the capability to connect to the Internet and provide you with everything you need to know about shipping a prospective item via most major professional carriers. Familiarize yourself with the rules and special features of each carrier so that you can make prudent shipping choices. Also use *stamps.com* to print your own postage labels and receive free delivery confirmation.

A SHIPPING PHILOSOPHY

Packing is labor intensive. Having the correct materials on hand and easy access is important to save time and money. Likewise, without proper equipment, the job can be more arduous and protracted. Customers may not buy from your business again and discourage others, if they have had a less than satisfactory shipping experience. Besides conducting your business in a professional manner, you must create a professional image as well. An entrepreneur must present a good first impression with each customer. *Will Rogers* once said, "You never get a second chance at a first impression."

GUERILLA GARAGE SALES

When it comes to customer-relations management, you cannot fix what you do not know. Therefore, the foundation of my shipping philosophy is the *Golden Rule*. This principle should be the bedrock of your business philosophy, especially the shipping standards to which you adhere. How can you sell unto others the same way you want to be treated, you may ask? Come around the sales counter and pretend you are the customer. Imagine the way *you* would prefer to be treated if someone was sending the same item to you. Then, vow to treat others the way *they want to be treated*. If you are unable to visualize yourself in someone else's situation, consider how you would treat a family member or a loved one under the same circumstances. You must put your customers first and give them what they want. Under this philosophy you package and ship a two-dollar item no differently than a $100-dollar item. Frankly, under no circumstance after the sale can you afford to simply dump the merchandise in a box, slap on a label, and ship it whenever you "get around to it." You would not do this to your mother or favorite uncle. Above all, it is important to package and ship your products in an efficient and reliable manner, because, fast and inexpensive shipping leads to customer satisfaction. And, you will not be successful unless your customers are satisfied and have a good experience. Customers don't care how much you know, it's mainly how much you *care*. From day one of your business launch, promise the least and *deliver* the most. That is why my basic philosophy is governed by the *Golden Rule*—it never goes out of style. Take the leap or be prepared to suffer the plunge. Deliver the goods—*NOW*.

XV

SPLITTING YOUR FORCE

Internet commerce from its earliest beginnings has been mainly confined to consumer-to-consumer transactions. On any given day, the auction giant, eBay, has five million items for sale. At last count, this site has over 22.5 million registered users. Today, however, the majority of people registered on eBay are buyers, not sellers. That means most users are sitting on the sidelines. This circumstance presents another opportunity for an enterprising entrepreneur to take the initiative, make some money, and help other people get rid of their stuff at the same time. You can serve as a *middleman* for those who want to sell their items online by handling the transaction for them. In effect, you will be selling on *consignment*. Not everyone has the energy or the talent to find and assess products, research condition and value, photograph, write descriptions, list the items for sale, and deal with the public. The process intimidates many people. They either fail to have the time, online access, or the savvy to trade on the Net, but they are willing to pay someone else to do it for them. Maybe they cannot master the complexity of the transactions or lack the ability to perform the many tasks that are necessary to operate an online business. The situation is ideal for a garage-sale-guerilla. Based upon the recent sales figures for eBay and other auction sites, I believe the inescapable conclusion is that an untapped supply of merchandise remains sitting in people's homes. The Internet marketplace has emerged into a middleman's dream, an opportunity to hook up an unlimited number of sellers and buyers directly with each other. No matter where you live, there are thousands of potential customers in your area who will pay you to sell their belongings. You have to find them, find a need, and fill it. A lot of people

GUERILLA GARAGE SALES

try to make money on the Internet, but have no idea how to sell or what to sell. You now know instinctively what people really want and how to efficiently merchandise. The Net auction business can be mastered quickly. Start by selling small and practice until you raise your skill level. Nonetheless, you must master some basic guerilla concepts before acting as a middleman.

As an entrepreneur, understand you are not merely selling *on* the Internet—you are selling *from* the Internet. This means you should not overlook all of the general marketing sales tools and other methods salesmen have perfected over the years to move their products. Just because you are on the Net does not mean you do not have *to sell* your product. All of the rules applicable to selling remain unaltered online with few exceptions. Selling requires your sincere effort. Internet selling is time consuming and like most enterprises you get back in large measure what you invest. The main advantage of the Net is that your products are exposed to a far wider audience than any other vehicle or medium. Before you can sell your products online for someone else, however, you have to sell yourself. Prior to spending any money with you a potential buyer will decide if you are trustworthy. The buyer may reside thousands of miles from your location. If you make the sale, he is going to send you money for something you agree to send him later. Your reputation, or the lack of it, is the deciding factor. Every aspect of your marketing plan must reassure your buyer that you are reliable. Your ads, correspondence, and offerings to potential customers should convey knowledge, sincerity, and credibility. Do not participate in "puffing" or make outrageous claims about your merchandise. If buyers do not believe what you say, they will not do business with you. The same thing is true about anyone who would allow you to sell for them. A large measure of credibility can be attained with a good "feedback" rating. They may also want to see your sales portfolio of items you have handled in the past. Furthermore, you must be creative and make your ads interesting to elicit an emotional response to prompt others to do business with you.

After satisfying this key question you must find a need and fill it. Sell online what people want to buy—items they cannot easily get elsewhere. As a middleman, you are in a position to choose the sellers you represent and what items you sell. In prior chapters we discussed the relationship of time and money. It takes about the same amount of time to sell a $500.00 item as it does something worth $50.00. Obviously, just considering the time factor, you want to sell higher priced items. Although I have not handled a large number of consignments, I also know the human element in dealing with buyers and sellers bears no reasonable relationship to the price of the item. If you are going to take about the same amount of flak from the public in connection with the $50.00 item, I recommend selling the more expensive merchandise. How do you make money selling on consignment? How do you minimize the problems that arise whenever you deal with the public? In a nutshell, here are some of the basics to help you become a competent middleman.

Before taking on the first consignment decide how you want to handle each transaction. Prepare a detailed handout to the prospective seller. Set forth the terms and conditions of sale, including a description of the services you provide, how you will represent the Seller, and all transactional fees. Have legal counsel prepare a simple written contract form for your everyday use. *Every client* should sign the contract before you initiate the consignment at any level. Have a portfolio of prior sales and a list of customers for references to provide each prospective client. Provide an information sheet for each seller to fill out and give basic data for preparation of the consignment contract, and the online listing ad, to sell their item.

The minimum information you will need to make a consignment is as follows:

⊕ Seller's name and address

⊕ Item description, including name, model, serial number, and size

⊕ Comprehensive unvarnished condition of item (Seller responsible for providing complete and correct information)

⊕ Original packaging (or not)

⊕ Seller's minimum sales price in U.S. dollars

⊕ Seller's telephone number and e-mail address

⊕ Paperwork, manuals, sales, and other documentation

GUERILLA GARAGE SALES

- Age of item

- Artist or manufacturer

- Provenance and history of the item

- Is the item unique in any way? Autographed?

The terms and condition of consignment should generally provide:

- Agreement that property is owned in fee simple by Seller and is not pledged or being otherwise sold by Seller

- Seller will not bid directly or indirectly on item during listing

- Whether you will sell faux, irregular, knockoff, reproductions; or only authentic items

- Who will maintain possession of the item (I prefer to keep possession to answer questions from buyers, verify condition, prepare the ad, and ship promptly)

- Who will respond to questions and provide buyer information (I do)

- Responsibility for damage or loss (Seller)

- Who will collect payment and handle accounting functions (I am responsible)

- When the Seller will be invoiced following the sale

- What fees and costs of consignment are to be paid by Seller

- Who is responsible for ad layout and design (I am)

- Who decides the auction features to utilize in listing the item for sale

- Who will post feedback (I do)

- Who ultimately determines the selling price (I do)

- Who photographs the object and decides the number of pictures to use (I do)

- Who will package and ship after the sale (I do)

- How and when is Seller paid after the sale

- Whether the Seller may cancel the sale once the item is listed (no)

- When the Buyer is not satisfied with the item, how are adjustments made, and who is responsible financially (Seller)

- How disputes between parties are settled

- How will item re-listing be conducted

Consignment selling is a good way to pick up extra income on the Internet. The largest negative for this type of selling is that you become a mini-business, and lose control of your time. If you are just selling for yourself, you can eBay or not. If you are soliciting items to sell as a middleman, you are in the consignment *business*. People will come to you with certain expectations and you will have to perform. If a conflict arises, *the customer comes first!* If you choose to become a serious middleman, at some point you will have to discontinue your personal online selling. The online marketplace is very specialized and can be difficult. Remember to collect all eBay or other third party fees up front before you list online. If the item does not sell, you will be personally responsible for these fees. Unless you become proficient and maintain a stable of worthwhile customers who bring you good assortment of expensive merchandise, you could find this type of selling more of a hassle than it is worth. But, if you can list automobiles, motorcycles, motor homes, expensive cameras, like this one

and other valuable items, you can generate a good income from a small number of listings each month. Finally, be certain to obtain good legal advice from a business attorney. You should have a contract to do business prepared by a lawyer, not anyone else. In most states you cannot charge a sales *commission* for selling motor vehicles, airplanes, or real estate without a broker's license, so be certain to retain a lawyer to explain the legal implications of consignment selling before you start. Good hunting!

SECTION THREE:

THE ELECTRONIC AD AND SELLING ON THE INTERNET

DAWN OF THE INTERNET

Anyone over 30 who is computer proficient, will most likely relate without hesitation, that *Al Gore* did not create the Internet. But if you ask them who invented the first computer, almost to a person the response will be a deafening credit to a group of scientists and employees at IBM, who actually developed such a device in the early 1950's, widely acclaimed as the world's first functional computer. They would all be wrong. The fact there are personal computers today, the Internet even exists, and most of the world does not speak German or Japanese as a first language, is a tribute to a dedicated "army" of British scientists, code breakers, and mathematicians who created the world's first programmable electronic computer in 1943. Built during the height of World War II, and dubbed "Colossus," this enormous machine was the size of a small room. It weighed more than a ton. It was created and brought to bear on behalf of the Allied war intelligence effort in a secret location 50 miles northwest of London at Bletchley Park. Ten thousand people worked around the clock throughout the war, breaking ciphers such as the German Enigma Code and other secret communiqués used by the Axis powers. The German Enigma Code was so sophisticated that each time a key was pressed on a machine to select a letter it could be communicated to another decoding machine in over one hundred and fifty million different ways. Furthermore, the Enigma Code settings were changed every eight hours to further complicate detection. In spite of a massive, persistent effort by the British, the German High Command had no clue its top secret military communications had been compromised, and continued to remain secure in the mistaken belief its coded messages were unbreakable during the entire course of the war. At war's end, all evidence of the Colossus program, including hardware, blueprints, and other documentation was destroyed on specific orders issued by Prime Minister *Winston Churchill*. Code-named "Ultra," its very existence and operation were classified by the British Government, and it remained a classified secret, not to be revealed for over 30 years, until declassified in the 1970's. This probably explains why most people today credit IBM with computer development. Although it was not documented in any history books until recently, the enormity of Colossus' contribution to the war effort will never be fully appreciated. At the very least it shortened the war by several years and spared thousands of Allied casualties. At best it saved Western Civilization from *Adolph Hitler*, the Nazis, and the Empire of Japan. Even by today's computing standards, Colossus was a scientific triumph and powerful analytical tool. It could decode 5,000 characters a second and the entire process took hours rather than weeks to compute.

Colossus saved our world from tyranny. Modern information technology began four decades ago. The great grandchildren of Colossus lead to development of the worldwide web that in turn launched the information age. Not since the dawn of the Industrial Revolution has life in industrial and post-industrial societies been characterized by such a major breakthrough in the advancement of information technology. Never before has so much data been available to human enterprise. In a quiet and relentless way, information technology is altering our world so profoundly that the movement dwarfs the changes brought on by Colossus' introduction of the computer to the world at war in 1943. In this age of instant communication and digital electronics, this development can yield large financial rewards to any entrepreneur who can master it. Rest assured, we're watching history in the making. Make your own history.

I

GETTING FROM THE FLEA MARKET TO THE INTERNET

Business is definitely hardball. In the battle for customers every sale matters. Historically, commerce has been dominated by large companies with unlimited resources, capital, and access to technology the likes of which smaller concerns could only dream. Given the incredible change in pace of all things, technology is empowering entrepreneurs. The Web is rapidly becoming the most cost effective means to reach potential customers—it lets little companies be global, and is the great equalizer. The image of the behemoth mega-chain-store as a relentless predator to everything in its path, bent on annihilation of smaller and vulnerable business prey is not necessarily the norm on the Internet. In biblical times when Goliath challenged the young David it hardly seemed a fair fight; the boy only had a puny slingshot and a prayer. Today, in cyberspace both David and Goliath companies put their modems on the same way, one bit at a time. Consequently, the "Davids" of the world can compete very effectively against the "Goliaths" of the industry, because everyone has access to current advances and new technology, which levels the playing field in cyberspace considerably. Furthermore, on the Web you are positioned for future technological advancements. Technology has been advancing at such a fast pace it seems almost impossible to keep up. We are living in an on-demand world. The small business "David" will probably never slay the corporate Giant "Goliath" on the Internet with a perfect stone. In the business world it takes a much bigger arsenal to accomplish that kind of feat. But, smaller businesses can take advantage of their stature by positioning themselves in a particular niche or where "Goliath" is handicapped i.e., making interpersonal business relationships, and providing one-on-one service. Moreover, smaller companies can change direction faster than larger ones. According to *John Buchanan*, Senior Vice President of Lettuce Entertain You Enterprises, "Entrepreneurs have confidence and are willing to gamble. Corporate types won't do that. They need validation." The "Goliaths" of the information technology world may never be the only solution; there have been too many "Davids" over the years working tirelessly on the Internet advancing the information revolution. With this in mind, it is easy to see and understand that in the end, besides his size, Goliath is remembered only for his defeat.

II

THE BEGINNING—TRY EBAY

A logical place to begin your Internet business is eBay. If you are already a registered eBay buyer or seller, then you can bypass this section. However, if eBay is totally new to you or you want a different user ID in order to sell on eBay, then this section is for you.

Before you can transact anything on eBay (including bidding or selling) you must first register. After you complete the registration process, you may set up a seller's account or become ID verified.

STEP 1: REGISTERING ON EBAY

When attempting to register, go to the eBay home page at www.ebay.com and click on Register at the top of the page, and fill in the fields of the electronic form. The first few questions are basic information: name, address, telephone numbers, and e-mail address. Toward the bottom of the page, eBay also asks you to create a User ID and password. Your User ID is like an online Social Security number that distinguishes you from the rest of the world. Your first reaction may be to use your unique e-mail address as your User ID. It is a good idea however, eBay will not allow it. Therefore, try to choose a designation that relates to what you are selling. For example, if you are a bookseller your User ID may be avidreader121. Or, if you have a certain hobby or like to collect coins, your User ID may be something like coinman25. Whatever handle you may choose, keep it simple in order for potential repeat customers to remember you in the future.

Now, you need to choose a password. Most people may not put much thought into their selection, but it is particularly important. If your password should fall into the wrong hands, the culprit not only has access to your credit card and bank account information, but he could affect your auctions and ruin your reputation and relationships with customers. Therefore, do not choose your password lightly, and never use the same one on multiple websites. Create unique passwords for each site, and change them occasionally before problems arise. Be creative, and use combinations of letters and numbers for maximum protection. For example your confirmation Bible verse "John 3 16" would work as your password unless you are a minister, or your name is John and you were born on March 16. Moreover, using your initials and birthday might be easy to remember, however, the password "grs122551" would self-destruct once someone learns your name is Gary Smith from the return address label, or your "Payable to" information. It would not be a difficult leap for someone to then conclude your middle initial is R, and you were born December 25, 1951. Suddenly, your password is compromised and the door to your world is wide open! At the conclusion of filling out the form and submitting it, you will receive an e-mail to confirm that you do indeed receive messages at that e-mail address. Once you confirm your e-mail address, your eBay account is activated.

STEP 2: BECOMING ID VERIFIED

In addition to registering as an eBay member, you may wish to become ID Verified. With this option, you can create your proof of identity and begin the process of establishing your trust as an honest seller in the eBay community. The ID Verify process registers your proof of identity and takes only about 10 minutes to complete by "verifying" your personal information and cross-checking against consumer and business databases for consistency. You will have to enter personal information such as your name and date of birth, as well as identify certain installment and credit accounts and their associated monthly payments. You will also have to provide your social security and driver's license number. There are certain restrictions with this option, however. Once you successfully pass ID Verify scrutiny, a $5 fee will be charged to your eBay account. Moreover, ID Verify is only available to residents of the United States and the U.S. territories Puerto Rico, US Virgin Islands, and Guam. You must provide your home address and personal information to pass the online verification process (work address and other contact information is not accepted).

III

NAVIGATING THE EBAY WEBSITE

Before you begin to sell on eBay, spend a little time to familiarize yourself with the website. At the top of the eBay home page are twelve words that will allow you operate, come and go, and perform any function on the eBay site. The links on the top row are *Home, Pay, Register, Site Map,* and *Search/Advanced Search.* Bottom row links include: *Buy, Sell, My eBay, Community, Help,* and *Sign In / Sign Out.*

HOME

The Home link is a useful tool because it takes you back to the eBay starting page from any other web page on the eBay website. No matter how lost or where you may be, once you click on the *home* link you will rejoin the eBay main page.

PAY

This link is maintained for customers to pay for their eBay purchases, not eBay sellers.

REGISTER

Using this link will allow you to register on eBay as a buyer or a seller.

SITE MAP

Are you still confused and unable to find what you are looking for? Are there just too many links and possibilities on the eBay home page? Make the Site Map your next destination. Every available link and service is provided for you, in easy to access, organized columns.

SEARCH/ADVANCE SEARCH

This tool is one of the most important devices for buyers and sellers. Just type in what you are looking for in the box and hit Search or click on the Advanced Search link underneath for more options. For the buyer, this link offers a variety of ways in which to search for an item:

- ✠ Category
- ✠ Payment Option
- ✠ Price
- ✠ Location
- ✠ Keyword or Item Number
- ✠ Seller
- ✠ Bidder
- ✠ eBay Stores

This tool can also be used by the seller to research eBay item prices. Just because you have a book that retails for $24.00 does not mean you will achieve the same price for it on eBay. How do you ascertain a competitive market price? The answer is by researching the item price and checking competitor prices; you can find all of this information here.

BUY

This tool is used primarily by buyers who are "surfing" with no particular product or category in mind. It provides a systematic way to search for items in several different ways, including:

- Category
- eBay Stores
- Themes
- Regions
- Common Keywords, and
- Featured Items

Moreover, a buyer can also conduct a search in *Featured Items*, which is a very useful tool for sellers as well! The seller has the option of using *eBay Listing Upgrades and Promotional Tools* to market any of his listed items. One of these upgrades is *Featured Plus*. With this option, you get double exposure. In fact, items using *Featured Plus* are 28% more likely to sell!

SELL

What you see is what you get. By using the *Sell Your Item Form* and answering simple questions with easy, accessible forms, this tool takes all of the hard part out of the selling equation. Best of all, after your first listing with this feature, you will have the option of saving your preferences so each new listing afterwards will already have the information filled in. This topic will be discussed in much more detail later.

Before you begin selling your products on eBay, I recommend browsing the *Selling Resources* at the bottom of the page. Not only does it offer information on *Getting Started*, but it also provides access to an insightful *How To Sell Tour*. Moreover, each resource is organized into easily accessible columns, including:

- Best Practices
- Seller Community
- Selling Solutions
- Advanced Selling
- Building Your Business
- Selling Supplies
- Seller News
- Third Party Services
- My eBay

MY EBAY

This tool is pivotal for both the buyer and seller! My eBay is a powerful set of tools that helps you track and manage all your eBay buying, selling, account information, preferences, and more! Not only does it allow the buyer to keep track of all bids, purchases, auctions, and any items that they are interested in, but it also permits the seller to track listings, unsold items, and sales. The following is a breakdown of the *My eBay features*:

✠ My Summary: The area where you can view all of your selling and purchasing activity, along with updates and announcements from eBay.

✠ All Buying: Allows you to manage your bids, items you are watching, buying totals, and items you did not win.

✠ All Selling: Manage everything you are selling, by tracking sales, sending payment invoices and reminders to your buyers, and keeping track of your unsold items.

✠ My Messages: Receive alerts and updates from eBay, as well as messages and questions from other eBay users.

✠ All Favorites: Choose your favorite categories, searches, and eBay sellers. Even have eBay e-mail you when new items matching your search requirements appear.

✠ My Account: Manage your account settings, including updating personal information, eBay preferences, feedback, seller account information, and PayPal account information all from one place. Also, change your *eBay Preferences* by placing unique settings for using and viewing My eBay and/or eBay as a whole. Furthermore, you can manage your *Feedback* by finding all the transactions for which you need to leave feedback, or view the feedback recently received.

✠ My Reviews & Guides: Read and write reviews for books, movies, CD's, and more. View guides to research more products and receive more in-depth knowledge.

GUERILLA GARAGE SALES

✠ Dispute Console: Manage and receive recourse by reporting unpaid items, non-paying bidders, and items not received or not as described.

COMMUNITY

This is the perfect way to keep in touch with eBay users and abreast of all the new changes and updates occurring almost every day. This tool will also help you to participate in the eBay community. The eBay Community can be broken down into the following:

✠ News and Announcements: Receive and learn about the latest news and new occurrences on eBay, including latest policy changes, new features, changes in fee structure, updates, and special offerings.

✠ Discussion, Help, & Chat: Use the Community Help and Discussion Boards on eBay to learn useful eBay tips and make lifelong eBay acquaintances. You may even learn some new marketing techniques, or receive answers to specific questions about a wide range of subjects, just by asking another *eBay user.*

✠ Education: Attend workshops, learn from an eBay mentor, and develop your eBay buying and selling skills.

✠ Marketplace Safety: Report transaction problems and safety concerns, as well as finding resources and tips on how to have a safe online experience.

✠ Sending Suggestions to eBay: Have any ideas or changes that you think should be made? Now is your chance to let eBay know, by sending them a confidential e-mail. They may or may not respond to your suggestions.

HELP

Have a question? Need an answer? When you are just starting out, this is a good source of information. You can access the entire eBay database for answers to all of your important questions. Start by clicking on the *Help Topics* at the top of the page, or if you have a specific question just type it in the *Search Help* box. If after all of this you are still looking for an answer, then you can contact eBay by clicking on *Contact Us* to the left of the page. The company promises a response turnaround in 24-48 hours. You can also visit the eBay *Community Answer Center* for chat rooms and to receive answers from other eBay members.

SIGN IN / SIGN OUT

Every time you need to log into your eBay account, you will have to use *Sign In* by giving eBay your User ID and password. For security purposes, your password is automatically encrypted by eBay every time you enter the site. Furthermore, whenever you want to leave the eBay website, always click on the *Sign Out* link so no one else can access your information.

IV

RESEARCH ON EBAY

The whole world is about making things and selling things. According to Dieringer Research Group, a Milwaukee market researcher, a majority of American adults are now using the Internet for shopping. We have already discussed the need to develop and implement a strategic marketing plan for your business if you want to successfully sell on the Internet. To dramatically increase your sales however, you need to go one step further. To better develop your overall income potential, you will have to do research. Go to eBay and analyze the sales history of an item. Do you know why one widget sells and a seemingly identical one does not sell? Have you ever compared the final price of one item only to discover under *eBay Completed Items* that another seller sold the same type of widget a short time later for a much higher price, or a lower price? If you discount timing, quality, or condition of the product, the answer is *writing Internet descriptions that sell*. Unless you discover a cure for the common cold, products do not normally sell themselves. You certainly need viable products to sell, but to a great extent *how* you list and advertise an item on the Internet will determine your potential profits, and whether or not you generate a healthy, consistent sales record for your business. The first impression a potential buyer and his computer will encounter, is the title and description that you advertise to list your widget. Before you can list anything for sale you have to research its marketability and worth by analyzing *comparable sales*. RESEARCH! RESEARCH! RESEARCH!

STEP 1: PRICING PAYOFF

When pricing an item on eBay, it is always best to know the success rate of other eBay sellers listing this particular item. To accomplish this step, go to the eBay homepage and type the name of your particular item at the top right portion of the Search Box, or in the big box at the left of the page. For example, for *The DaVinci Code* you would type this title in the box at the left. All the current listings for *The DaVinci Code* on the eBay site will unfold, sorted in the time ending soonest. To change the sort order of the listings, click on Sort by and choose from the following: *ending soonest, newly listed, lowest price, highest price, nearest location*, and *PayPal payment option*. If you choose the nearest location option, you will be prompted to enter your zip code. eBay will then organize the listings by distance and report the mileage separating each listings from your location.

The lowest price and highest price sorting options are also a very handy tool when it comes to calculating the price of your item.

By viewing the caption above, I know the listing with the highest bid price is $10.50, while the lowest is $5.99. Also, unless autographed by the Author or some other significant factor, I can infer that the listing at $15.00 is above the maximum price that a customer is willing to pay. However, before I put my money on the line, I need to conduct a little more research. Why do the two books in the $10.00 range have bids but not the lower-priced one at

$5.99? To answer this question, I simply click on each of the listings to find out more information. This is what the $10.50 listing looks like:

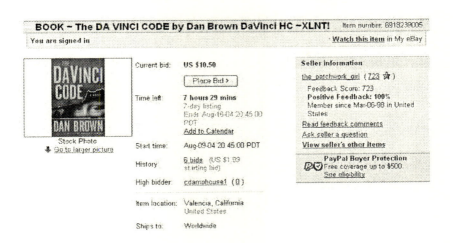

Mystery solved! You can now see why this seller's listing is receiving bids. First, in the item description, the condition of the item is "new". (The listing at $5.99 is in "very good" condition.) Thus, the condition of the item has a very big effect on the price. Secondly, the $10.50 seller has a high feedback transaction score of 723, with a perfect 100% positive feedback rating. I cannot over-emphasize that a seller's feedback rating can be his best friend, or worst enemy. It is the only way of revealing a seller's reputation online. This communicates several things to potential bidders. The high feedback score indicates that he is not a new seller and he has participated in enough transactions to have a viable selling reputation with the buying public. Also, because this seller has maintained a 100% feedback rating, a bidder will feel more comfortable doing business with him because there is a strong perception of less risk with this dealer. Feedback is discussed in more detail under the "Chatter" chapter in this book. The third point that makes this seller's listing more marketable is the inclusion of a sharp picture of the item in the ad. As you are aware, over 80% of eBay listings that have a picture sell over the rest. It comes down to basic psychology; a customer wants to see the goods in advance of their purchase. Another reason why this $10.50 listing is more attractive stems from its bidding history. The starting bid for this item was $1.99. Frequently, a low starting price will entice more than one bidder to make an offer. When this happens, a bidding war may precipitate, and the final price often escalates! Further, this seller is more appealing because his shipping area is worldwide. This gives him a competitive advantage with a much broader audience, and considerably more exposure than someone shipping exclusively in the continental United States or only several countries. Obviously shipping may not have anything to do with the ultimate bid price, but increased market exposure adds to the seller's chances of making a sale. (When you consider defining your shipping territory, please read the section on logistical support and acquire some firsthand experience with foreign shipping before you make a final decision). This item's increased sales potential is further boosted by the seller's payment methods. He accepts PayPal, the world's largest online banking system, and a subsidiary of eBay. By accepting PayPal, he gives the winning bidder two convenient ways to pay. He can pay with his credit card or by an e-check. Furthermore, the seller is able to accept several different credit card brands, including MasterCard, Visa, and Discover. More importantly, by accepting PayPal, the winning bidder's purchase is covered up to $500.00, assuring a smooth transaction for both the buyer and seller.

STEP 2: SURVEY COMPLETED ITEMS

We might never know why an item sells, but there is a way for you to view the completed listings (up to several weeks) to check out any item and get some idea. Go to the *Search Options* box to the left of the page and place a checkmark on *Completed listings*. (Note: if you are currently not signed in, you will be prompted to do so. To sign in, you must be an eBay member with a valid User ID and password.)

This page has the same sorting options and other menu alternatives as the current listings page. This is distinct and helpful because it catalogues items that have ended, whether they sold, and if so, the final sales price and other pertinent information. When using this tool, do not merely scan the prices and make an assumption from

GUERILLA GARAGE SALES

this one bit of data. Dig a little deeper. Click on individual listings to discern exactly what was listed and sold by the seller, and how the ad was constructed. Look to see if there was a picture (and analyze the picture), what payment options were accepted, the condition of the item, bidding history, and the seller's feedback rating. Any of these points can vastly affect the pricing of an item. Ignoring or underestimating even one of these factors can result in no bids and a loss of profit.

V

SELL YOUR ITEM ON EBAY

Now that all of your research is complete, it is time to begin selling! Go to the eBay homepage and click on *Sell* at the top. This takes you to a new page where you can choose the selling format: online auction, fixed price, or real estate.

Initially, even when dealing with used merchandise, you must decide whether you have a unique item, or if you have ordinary merchandise. Non-unique property includes personal and household goods normally found in your local retail outlets. If your item is unique you may want to try the auction format, which usually generates more sales revenue. Everything else should generally be marketed in the "fixed price" category. In this format, the item will only sell at the stated price. Before you get too involved, the best course of action is to try selling for a while until you have a firm grasp of the *auction* and *fixed price* formats.

Auctions are crazy sometimes, and you might get lucky and sell something for many times its worth. Other times you might only break even or lose money. If you have confidence in your item though, start it out for auction at a low figure, like ninety-nine cents. This is an easy way to save on up-front listing fees. It is a very comforting feeling when you see several bidders raising the ante. However, do not be surprised if the auction ends with only one bid at the listing price, and you have a loss! But after you attain experience, this will happen less and less. Auctions can be a gamble. That is why you may want to set a pre-auction Reserve Price.

GUERILLA GARAGE SALES

STEP 1: Choosing a Category

Once you have chosen the listing format, it is time to pick a suitable category to list your item. eBay has hundreds of categories, with even more subcategories. Choosing one that is a match for your item can sometimes be time consuming. Again, my best advice is to research and determine the consensus category chosen by other sellers in the past. Data from Auction Software Review by RainWorx can point you in the right direction. According to their research accumulated during the period from November 24 to December 2, 2003, the following are the most popular categories on eBay, based on the number of items listed:

Category	Number of Items	% of Total Items
Collectibles	2,790,047	17%
Clothing and Accessories	1,752,844	11%
Entertainment	1,720,951	11%
Sports	1,509,556	9%
Home	1,326,249	8%
Jewelry & Watches	1,253,376	8%
Computers & Electronics	1,117,060	7%
Toys & Hobbies	1,085,657	7%
Books	752,467	5%
Everything Else	577,648	4%
Pottery & Glass	425,740	3%
Art	301,738	2%
Dolls & Bears	270,386	2%
Antiques	254,859	2%
Business & Industrial	221,857	1%
Coins	221,060	1%
Stamps	208,527	1%
Musical Instruments	162,931	1%
Tickets	34,769	0.22%
Specialty Services	24,866	0.16%
Travel	15,480	0.1%
Real Estate	2,108	0.01%
TOTAL	**16,030,176**	

Nevertheless, be aware that occasionally the process can be much more complicated. For example, what if you were selling a rare book on *WWII Weapons and Arms?* Your first instinct might be to list under the Book category. What about the *Militaria* category? Chances are if you did your homework, you would find that sellers have listed this item under both categories. Even more research might reveal which category was utilized the most and the best price attained, but there is another superior timesaving method available. eBay gives you the option to list under two categories at once. Therefore you could gain even more exposure by attracting both the book collector and the army veteran to your ad. The only downside is eBay doubles your insertion fee and final value fee in these instances. Nonetheless, if you are selling high-priced items and need a lot of exposure then this method can be invaluable.

Once you have completed your research and found the most suitable category, you complete your category listing with the applicable subcategories that best describe your item. Confusion may develop with subcategories, but the same multiple listing options apply to subcategories. There are usually several subcategories in outline form following the main category.

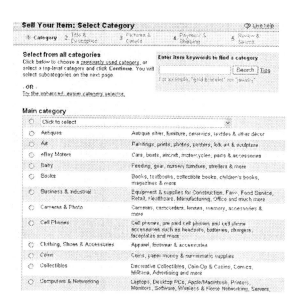

After experimenting with the default category selector, you may want to try the updated, enhanced version (only for Internet Explorer):

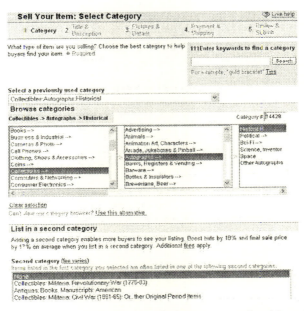

Depending on the type of item you are listing, you may be able to list with *Pre-Filled Item Information*. This option automatically fills in your listing with *Item Specifics* information when you enter a unique product identifier (ISBN, UPC, title, author, and artist). It can provide basic pre-written facts (book synopses, film credits, etc.) about your item and even provide a stock picture in some cases. Most importantly, this option allows you to save time writing your description and adding pictures while creating listings that are clear and appealing to buyers. However, you should still add your own description (along with the condition) to each item to personalize it further.

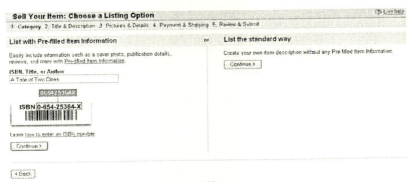

STEP 2: CREATING A TITLE AND ITEM SPECIFICS

If you choose not to list with *Pre-Filled Item Information* or are not given the option, you can continue listing the standard way. At this point you must draft the ad title. Do not try to be overly creative with your title, use puns, or cute clichés. Craft a title like it would appear in the classified section of your local newspaper. Space requirements dictate a short description of the item that comes right to the point, because eBay only allows you a limited number of characters (55, including spaces) in which to situate the title. Furthermore, the eBay search system uses exact matches, not "fuzzy searches". Bottom line, this means the item must be spelled correctly with full detail—all the i's are dotted and t's crossed. If the item is not described precisely in the title, or is misspelled, then the eBay search engine will not acknowledge it, nor will any prospective buyer ever see it. If you are a beginner, do not reinvent the wheel. If you draw a blank for your title, you can always research current and prior sales to draw inspiration from other sellers.

If given the option, you should also enter *Item Specifics* for the product that you are listing. This option is available for most eBay categories, and provides vital information to all potential buyers. If you are unsure of the item information, leave it blank. Nevertheless, it is better to answer what you do know, rather than leave the entire form blank.

Sell Your Item: Describe Your Item

1. Category   2. **Title & Description**   3. Pictures & Details   4. Payment & Shipping   5. Review & Submit

Item title *Required

    Charles Dickens A Tale of Two Cities FIRST EDITION

5 characters left, no HTML, asterisks, or quotes.
Include specific details about your item. Get tips on writing a good title. Learn More

Subtitle ($0.50)

    First Edition Hardcover Book with Dust Jacket

10 characters left.
Add a Subtitle (searchable by item description only) to give buyers more information. See example

---

Item specifics : Fiction Books

Category
    Classics

Special Attributes
    ☑ 1st Edition
    ☐ Signed
Condition
    Used
Format
    Hardcover
Publication Year
    1867

If you do not know the Publication Year, please leave blank.

STEP 3: AD COMPOSITION

After you have picked the category and drafted the title, the next step is the description, or body of the ad. At this juncture eBay does not limit the length of your ad copy and you can write as much as you wish. I do not want to oversimplify this process, but just like choosing a category and writing a title, there are certain tips you can follow to make your ad more powerful. Here are several ways to make your item description come to life. Quality is always better than quantity. In actuality, you have a limited amount of time and space to capture the prospective buyer when he clicks on your ad. You only have seconds to grab his attention or in the click of a mouse he will be gone to a competitor. Your layout needs to be interesting, colorful, and professional *with no misspelled words!* The copy needs to communicate quality, value, trust, and confidence. Imagine that you are writing an ad for an *infomercial* and the buyer has a remote control. Think of all the descriptive adjectives and adverbs you could bring to bear in describing your item to add a level of excitement. Whenever possible, try to make the prospective buyer interested in your product. Once again, the use of clichés and overused words is generally ineffective. Try words that apply only to your item. For example, if you are selling books you can use words like "out-of-print, first edition, or autographed by author." If you are selling electronics you can use words like "refurbished, brand new, factory sealed, or looks like it has never been used." When selling collectibles, "limited edition, or still in the original box" might be appropriate. Always make your ad appeal to the buyer. Communicate features and possible uses for the product. HTML (HyperText Markup Language) is one of the best ways to spice up your ad. eBay helps you do this with the *WYSIWYG* description editor on the eBay *Sell Your Item Form* (for Internet Explorer users only), located on the eBay website. This feature works just like a word processor. You can bold, italicize, underline, and change the font of your letters. Whenever you finish the WYSIWYG program and view the ad, it looks the same way a potential buyer will view it, hence the name *What You See Is What You Get*. Presently, the program only offers limited functional control and manipulation of text and backgrounds, and is available for *Internet Explorer* users only. It is therefore recommended that you learn some basic HTML:

To add a paragraph indent: <P> **Your Text Here**</P>
To add a break indent:
Your Text Here</>

To center your text:	<Center>**Your Text Here**</Center>
To bold your text:	<B>**Your Text Here**</B>
To italicize your text:	<I>**Your Text Here**<I>
To change font size:	
Large Font Size:	<font size=+2> **Your Text Here** </font>
Small Font Size:	<font size=-1> **Your Text Here** </font>
To add bullets:	<ul>
	<li>**Your Text Here**
	<li>**Your Text Here**
	<li>**Your Text Here**
	</ul>

HTML not only makes your ad look better but also easier to read. Instead of using indentions to start each new paragraph, it is more appealing to the human eye to insert a blank line (see how to add a paragraph indent above) and thus separate them for the reader. Moreover, try to use only a couple sentences per paragraph. Most people will not read long, verbose ads. If you have a lot of information you can always communicate it more effectively by a bulleted list (see above), shorthand versions, or only displaying key points. This makes your copy more readable and pleasing to the buyer's eye. Furthermore, be careful with your choice of type font and letter size. Using all caps is too hard to read and generally should be avoided. Unless it fits into your overall layout, do not include fancy fonts—stick with common, time-tested, readable lettering such as Arial, Times New Roman, and Courier. Experimenting with other fonts can distract the reader, detract from the overall appearance of your ad, and make copy difficult to read. Avoid pictures, images, sound, and music that take too long to load. Most web surfers are not going to wait more than a few seconds to view your presentation no matter how good it may be, and music can be annoying to some. Do not insert backgrounds or images that take away from your sales presentation. Using a dark text on a light background is usually the most effective approach, but not purple on a dark background. There is nothing wrong with the traditional white background with black text, or the reverse. In conclusion, what you say is the most important feature of advertising. A Picture, lettering, color, and background should only complement the language you select to communicate to your target audience. The lesson to be learned: words can lead to deeds.

Writing the ad for Internet Explorer users/non Internet Explorer:

STEP 4: CREATE AN AD TEMPLATE

Writing each ad on eBay is a lot of work! Depending on the item for sale, you can spend 10 to 30 minutes or longer just writing the description! One of the best laborsaving devices is to create a template for your eBay ad. Below is a sample of an ad template that I used for a book that recently sold on eBay:

You are bidding on <B>"A Stroll Through Modernista Barcelona"</B> brand new hardcover book!<P>
Book Information:
<UL>
<LI>ISBN: 84-343-0879-7
<LI>Photographer: Melba Levick
<LI>234 Full-Color Photographs
<LI>Original Spanish Text: Lluis Permanyer
<LI>Translator: Richard Rees
<LI>Printed: In Spain
<LI>Binding: Hardcover with Dust Jacket
</UL><P>
<B><Center>Synopsis:</B></Center>
<I><Center>Modernista</I> architecture was not only the product of the convictions of innumerable architects, but it also received the unconditional support of property owners. In the pages of this book we discover an array of astonishing works by following an itinerary designed to be both instructive and pleasurable. The result, a stimulating promenade, with none of the characteristics of a simple catalog, on which the reader will be able to discover, admire, and savor the best of <I>Modernisme.</I></Center><P>
<B>With over 230 stunning full-color photographs,</B> this hardcover book is in <B>brand new</B> condition!<P>

<A href="http://search.ebay.com/_W0QQsassZnphoffman"><B>Please See My Many Other Items Listed On eBay!!</B></A><P>
<B>Shipping and Payment Details:</B>
I prefer PayPal as payment option! But you can also pay with a money order, cashier's check, or personal check. Seller will wait until personal check clears before shipping. Buyer pays fixed shipping of $4.00 via USPS Media Mail, only in the Continental USA. I will also ship to an APO address for no extra charge. <B>Insurance is $1.30 extra!</B> I will combine on shipping. <B>If you have any questions, please e-mail me before bidding!</B> Thanks for your interest.

Just the addition of basic HTML, improves the look of the ad considerably. It is more professional and easier to read. This is the final product after the HTML fine-tuning:

GUERILLA GARAGE SALES

You are bidding on **"A Stroll Through Modernista Barcelona"** brand new hardcover book!

Book Information:

- ISBN: 84-343-0879-7
- Photographer: Melba Levick
- 234 Full-Color Photographs
- Original Spanish Text: Luis Permanyer
- Translator: Richard Rees
- Printed: In Spain
- Binding: Hardcover with Dust Jacket

Synopsis:

Modernista architecture was not only the product of the convictions of innumerable architects, but it also received the unconditional support of property owners. In the pages of this book we discover an array of astonishing works by following an itinerary designed to be both instructive and pleasurable. The result, a stimulating promenade, with none of the characteristics of a simple catalog, on which the reader will be able to discover, admire, and savor the best of *Modernisme*.

With over 230 stunning full-color photographs, this hardcover book is in **brand new** condition!

Please See My Many Other Items Listed On eBay!!

Shipping and Payment Details:
I prefer PayPal as payment option! But you can also pay with a money order, cashier's check, or personal check. Seller will wait until personal check clears before shipping. Buyer pays fixed shipping of $4.00 via USPS Media Mail, only in the Continental USA. I will also ship to an APO address for no extra charge. **Insurance is $1.30 extra!** I will combine on shipping. **If you have any questions, please e-mail me before bidding!** Thanks for your interest.

I have interspersed HTML bold in order to draw attention and make it more noticeable. The <B> **tells the text to be bold, and the** </B> tells it to go back to the normal text. The <I> *is used for italics*</I>.

The <BR> stands for break, and signifies the end of the line or sentence.

 is a double break, which skips a line. Moreover, I also used <P> to signify the beginning of a new paragraph. Always remember to use </P> at the end, otherwise all of your text will run together.

I also created bullets with the following text:
<UL>
<LI>Your Text Here
<LI>Your Text Here
<LI>Your Text Here
</UL>

To create your own hyperlink to direct buyers to your other items for sale, just copy my HTML, and change where it has my eBay user ID and substitute your own user ID. For example, if your eBay user ID is gameplayer101, then your hyperlink would look like this:

<Ahref="http://search.ebay.com/0QqsassZgameplayer101"><B>Please See My Many Other Items Listed On eBay!!</B></A>

In other words, the basic HTML for this particular hyperlink is:

<Ahref="http://search.ebay.com/ 0QqsassZenteruserid"><B>entertexthere</B></A>

STEP 5: PAYMENT AND SHIPPING CONDITIONS

After drafting the main body of the ad, it is time to include shipping and payment details. Before you begin to include shipping fees in your ad, you need to decide if you will be selling only in the Continental United States or internationally, and if so, which countries. Shipping internationally may not be a problem if you make the buyer pay all shipping costs, but remember that international shipments involve more paperwork. Depending on what you are selling you may need special customs papers and other paperwork required by your carrier. In fact, it can sometimes be such a hassle that many sellers do

GUERILLA GARAGE SALES

not operate outside the continental United States. Nonetheless, this is a big market and when you begin, you should try shipping overseas for a period of time. It is always a good idea to include the shipping costs up front in your ad. If for some reason you cannot announce your shipping costs in advance, then urge prospective buyers to leave their zip code and mailing address so you can provide a quote prior to the auction's close. Many eBay buyers are suspicious about over-priced shipping costs and you will lose a large portion of your audience if you do not provide specific expenses ahead of time in your ad. I personally decided to buy my own scale in order to weigh my items and download the latest shipping rates from the Post Office online. These "electronic scales" can cost from $50.00 to several hundred dollars. Besides the actual cost of shipping, I recommend charging a small fee for handling costs to cover expenses for packing material, operating costs, and overhead. Always include handling costs in your shipping quote in your ad, but keep it reasonable or it will adversely affect sales. After enumerating shipping costs, one should be certain to outline payment terms. The easier you make payment for customers, the more business you will attract. If you are selling internationally be sure to specify the currency you wish to receive along with rules on foreign checks or wire transfers. When selling in the United States include all of your payment options such as personal checks, cashier checks, and money orders, etc. Also include the deadline to receive payment after the auction's end and how long you will wait for checks to clear your financial depository. As a rule of thumb, for maximum effectiveness, your shipping and payment terms should not be longer than the rest of your ad. Draft your ad in clear, simple language and to the point. Avoid long verbose sentences and complex language. This can intimidate potential buyers and cost you business. Write for the village idiot so that anyone can easily understand what you are trying to convey.

STEP 6: TIMING YOUR AD FOR BEST RESULTS

You are almost finished! You have chosen a category, a title, written the ad description, and have included shipping and payment terms. But one of the most important listing components in your Internet ad is timing—when you start and end your auctions! The good thing about eBay is almost any time is a good time because eBay is global 24/7, which means a large audience is online all the time, every day. Nonetheless, there are certain times of the day that are better to list than others. Through experience I have found that it is more advantageous for me to launch my listings and have them end on a weekend rather than during the week. Most people have free time at home during weekends and are usually working or otherwise occupied the rest of the time. However, if your target audience is housewives this may not affect you, but you need to analyze this aspect carefully. Also the time of season can greatly impact sales. Selling bathing suits or school supplies in November might not be a good marketing strategy. Further, the time the listing concludes is just as important as the initial listing time. If you list your item at 1:00am, it will also end at 1:00am. The optimal or prime time for your listing to end is around 7:00 or 8:00pm at the latest. However, eBay is global and 7:00pm in Texas is not 7:00pm in Singapore. Presently, eBay gives you several choices for the length of your auction duration—1, 3, 5, 7, or 10 days. Decide which duration works best for you. You must experiment to determine the optimum timing pattern taking into account the goods you have to sell and your potential market, and then act accordingly. Once again, Auction Review Software statistics reveal how important the timing of your listing can be:

Seconds Won Before End	Number of Items	% of Total Items
0	2	0.1%
1	28	2.0%
2	1	0.1%
3	8	0.6%
4	1	0.1%
5 to 10	53	3.8%
11 to 20	53	3.8%
21 to 30	27	1.9%
31 to 45	31	2.2%
46 to 60	11	0.8%
TOTAL	**215**	**15%**

This data was tabulated from a sample of 3,500 auctions which deleted all items receiving zero bids, or were acquired by *Buy It Now*, leaving 1,413 auctions. Of this sample, 215 were won in the last 60 seconds. The above table pinpoints when these auctions ended. There is no right or wrong way, just some bids and more bids.

VI

REGISTERING ON PAYPAL

After you register on eBay, I recommend that you also sign up for a PayPal account. Just like eBay, registering and creating an account on PayPal is *gratis*. To access the site, just go to www.paypal.com.

PART 1: WHAT IS PAYPAL?

When I listed my first Internet auction lot for sale on eBay over five years ago, I began receiving pre-transaction questions from potential buyers inquiring about payment options. I was frequently asked if I accepted buyer payment from Billpoint and PayPal. Until that moment I had never heard of these concerns. After inquiry I was surprised to learn that these corporations, and others like them, existed almost solely as an online payment processor enabling millions of vendors and purchasers to conduct business on the Internet. Likewise, I soon learned that a majority of buyers wanted to access this type of pay service as an integral part of Internet commerce. Some buyers boldly insisted on this option or no sale. I was astounded to discover that the patron accessing the service was not charged—it was my responsibility as the seller! At first I was miffed. Even though my customer for some unknown reason could not pay me conventionally by check or money order, some company I never knew existed was going to charge me a fee! And, I was never consulted! Then it dawned on me. Every potential purchaser could control this aspect of the sales equation and force me to pay for their credit convenience. That was over 8,500 transactions ago.

PART 2: WHY WOULD A SELLER ACCEPT PAYPAL?

A subsidiary of eBay, PayPal is the fastest and easiest way to accept payments for your eBay listings. In fact, almost 70% of eBay listings accept PayPal as their payment option. eBay even has its own search category for listings that accept PayPal. What this means is that some potential customers may bypass your listing completely if you do not accept PayPal as your payment option. It is the quickest way to accept credit card payments and electronic checks online. As a seller, you can now get paid for your eBay listings faster—no waiting for checks or money orders to arrive in the mail. The buyer can now pay with his credit card in a matter of minutes and you will receive payment in a matter of seconds! This means that you can ship his item right away. Thus, you have taken care of several problems: you know you have been paid, you can ship the buyer's item as soon as possible, and you will receive positive Feedback for fast shipping. As well as allowing you to accept credit card payments, PayPal also provides several functional seller tools:

Add PayPal logo to your auction: Lets your buyers know that you accept credit cards through PayPal by including a PayPal logo in your listing.

Invoice your buyer: PayPal Winning Buyer Notification (WBN) automatically sends an e-mail invoice to your buyer. WBN e-mails include all of the information your winning buyers will need to pay, including a link back to the item listing, and a PayPal payment button.

Manage eBay items sold: PayPal's Post-Sale Manager tracks payments, invoices, shipments, and feedback from one location, thus allowing you to manage and organize all of your auctions.

Shipping and tracking tools: Whether you ship your auction items with the U.S. Postal Service or UPS—you can pay for shipping, print shipping labels, and track packages from your PayPal account.

Manage PayPal payments: Allows you to import your transaction history to money management software and create sales reports.

PART 3: HOW DOES PAYPAL WORK?

PayPal is an online payment service enabler with over 50 million registered account users. Even though it looks like a bank, acts like a bank and sounds like a bank, according to the Federal Deposit Insurance Corporation, PayPal is not a bank or savings association "because it is not chartered and

GUERILLA GARAGE SALES

does not accept *deposits* as defined by federal law." Moreover, "PayPal does not physically handle or hold funds placed into the PayPal service," the FDIC said in an advisory letter mailed to PayPal over two years ago. The company is licensed in many states as a money transmitter not a bank, and is *not* required to comply with customary state or federal banking laws. A new word was coined to describe how PayPal differs from most traditional financial institutions. Nicknamed "beaming" this web-based exchange of a new form of money is technically not transferred between individuals like a bank, it *beams* funds from one PayPal account to another because every participant was required to be a member. The basic service is free as long as you are the buyer or have a *Personal Account*. Although the exchange of funds is immediate and reasonably secure, this slight distinction separates PayPal from most financial service institutions subject to normal banking requirements whereby funds are transferred directly to a user. With PayPal an actual legal transfer of funds contemplated by banking regulations does not occur until an account holder actually moves funds from their PayPal account to their local bank or they formally request PayPal to send them a check withdrawing funds from their account. Besides providing personal e-mail accounts, PayPal also offers online business accounts, auction payments, and web accounts.

PayPal was acquired by e-Bay in October of 2002 even though eBay's subsidiary, *Billpoint*, had been a major competitor in the online payment service business. Subsequently, eBay merged its Billpoint and PayPal operations and retained only the PayPal brand. Since PayPal is not a bank or savings association, individual account holders are not directly afforded benefits, safeguards, or protection which conventional institutions normally provide their customers, such as federal deposit insurance.

PART 4: HOW SECURE IS PAYPAL?

The major concern of online shoppers is safety and security. When purchasing something, consumers use PayPal instead of providing credit information to each online vendor. It is believed this method is safer, more secure, and convenient because likelihood of a breach of security is less when the credit information is stored with PayPal instead of multiple sites of individual sellers. In other words, with one account you can do business around the world with millions of sellers and only provide your account information once. PayPal.com prides itself on security and privacy afforded its site users. The following information is advertised on their security information page:

> *"PayPal automatically encrypts your confidential information in transit from your computer to ours using the Secure Sockets Layer protocol (SSL) with an encryption key length of 128 bits (the highest level commercially available). Before you even register or log in to our site, our server checks that you're using an approved browser – one that uses SSL 3.0 or higher. Once your information reaches us, it resides on a server that is heavily guarded both physically and electronically. Our servers sit behind an electronic firewall and are not directly connected to the Internet, so your private information is available only to authorized computers."*

In spite of this, I have had to change my password on at least one occasion because unauthorized third parties were attempting to negotiate my PayPal account and I recommend you consider a similar precautionary measure.

In the event you retain an account balance with PayPal you are informed by the company that your fund "may lose value." In plain language this means you could legally lose everything without much recourse. Although this probability might be low, you need to recognize this sobering possibility. The company allows you to hold a balance in two ways: "(1) PayPal, as your agent, will place your funds in a pooled account at an unaffiliated FDIC-insured bank or savings institution, which is eligible for pass-through FDIC insurance coverage; or (2) you can elect to earn a return on your funds by enrolling to invest all funds that you receive into the PayPal Money Market Fund." Like anything in the financial world, the above option with the highest rate of return offers less security, and the second option may afford little security. Moreover, neither option presently offered by the company grants the full protection benefits that are provided by your local bank or savings and loan. Even in the situation where you receive the benefit of FDIC pass-through insurance protection up to $100,000.00, your account is only protected from the *bank's* failure. Therefore, your account "may lose value," depending on PayPal record keeping, the findings of the FDIC as a *receiver*, or PayPal's unlikely *bankruptcy*. Until the company addresses these risks, I cannot endorse maintaining a sizeable account balance when there are many other fully secure alternatives that extend depositors a greater rate of return and complete relative safety.

GUERILLA GARAGE SALES

PART 5: PAYPAL PROS AND CONS

There are numerous benefits in utilizing this company. On the positive side PayPal is:

- a readily accessible site that allow you to pay for things or send money online instantly anywhere any time

- an international payment system with 56 million account members worldwide and available in 45 countries around the world

- available to any qualified individual who has an e-mail account

- free to become a member

- a subsidiary of and works hand in hand with eBay and its sales infrastructure

- a remarkable tool to assist consumers to pay for products online without divulging sensitive credit information to vendors

- easy to join and operate

- an automated service that notifies you instantly when you receive payments and notifies winning bidders immediately

- a global leader in online payments

- a system that allows the collection of subscription or recurring payments

- a service that allows consumers to accept credit card and/or bank account payments for single or multiple item purchases

- complementary of regular bank accounts

- a secure site that can be insured for further protection

183

PayPal negatives include:

- merchant accounts can be frozen until a problem can be resolved

- cannot shift PayPal fees to the buyer

- complaints may not be addressed as swiftly as other financial services companies

- it is difficult to have a dialogue with company representatives when problems arise

- you are paying money to receive money already owed

- funds do not have the protection of FDIC or FSLIC

- rate of return on deposits is not competitive nor as secure as other conventional financial alternatives

PART 6: OTHER ONLINE "BANKING" COMPANIES

Like any business model, PayPal has competition. The United States Postal Service has an online payment service. Western Union Bid Pay provides similar cash online services. There is also Yahoo Pay Direct and another company called ProPay.com you may want to investigate. Paymate is a similar service in Australia (not affiliated with PayPal). Outside of the United States AnyPay offers a different model utilizing transfers between bank accounts, similar to electronic checks. I have had no experience in receiving payment from any of these other alternative service providers.

PART 7: PAYPAL FEES

In human activity there is good and bad in everything. Just like the Force in "Star Wars", PayPal has a dark side—its fees. Keep in mind, it does not cost the buyer anything to send payment via PayPal; it only costs the seller to receive the payment when you set up a Premier/Business account. Of course PayPal only charges fees to keep their business running. You would have to pay a fee anyway to accept credit cards with any other credit card company,

GUERILLA GARAGE SALES

but still you are paying money to receive money. Is there a way around this? Yes there is—a right way and a wrong way. eBay policy specifically prohibits sellers from shifting the PayPal fee to the buyer. Therefore, always remember to avoid any discussion with any customer that could be construed as fee shifting. I charge a nominal shipping and handling fee up front on each transaction to cover a myriad of expenses, including PayPal charges. Moreover, when I list an item for sale I start the minimum bid slightly higher to cover expenses and overhead like PayPal. Here is an outline of *PayPal's Fee Schedule*:

Fees

PayPal charges Premier and Business accounts to receive payments. Personal Accounts are free, but may not receive debit or credit card payments.

	Personal Account	Premier/Business Account
Open an Account	Free	Free
Send Money	Free	Free
Withdraw Funds	Free for accounts in US Fees for other banks	Free for accounts in US Fees for other banks
Add Funds	Free	Free
Receive Funds	Free	1.9% to 2.9% + $0.30 USD+~
Multiple Currency Transactions	Exchange rate includes 2.5% fee*	

+ These fees apply to U.S. users only.

* If your transaction involves a currency conversion, it will be completed at a retail foreign exchange rate determined by PayPal, which is adjusted

CASH HOFFMAN

regularly based on market conditions. This exchange rate includes a 2.5% spread above the wholesale exchange rate at which PayPal obtains foreign currency, and the spread is retained by PayPal. The specific exchange rate that applies to your multiple currency transaction will be displayed at the time of the transaction.

~Does not apply to Website Payments Pro or Virtual Terminal.

I know the fees on PayPal may not seem like much, but over time these fees really add up. Annually I pay hundreds of dollars in PayPal's fees— money that could be spent on packing supplies or other business operation expenses! After hearing all of this, you may be wondering why you need to accept PayPal at all. It is not required, but keep in mind that over 70% of eBay auctions utilize the service. eBay even has a special search for auctions that accept PayPal. This means that you could be overlooking a huge percentage of potential buyers. Moreover, it is more convenient for you and the buyer. With his credit card, the buyer can pay you instantly and you can ship his item right away. No waiting for money orders in the mail or for checks to clear at the bank. Fast payment + fast shipment = great transaction + positive Feedback for both parties.

PART 8: PAYPAL IS HERE TO STAY

To understand how PayPal operates, you must realize it is a relatively new business model that paved the way for enlisted men like me to compete in the expanded universe of cyberspace. It is not a bank or credit card company, but more of a payment intermediary for e-business transactions. Because PayPal is a pioneer, the financial service industry and government regulators have had little impact on its business. Named the 2002 SIIA Codie Awards "Best eCommerce Solution," and recognized by *PC Magazine* as one of "The Top 100 Web Sites," in the short term the company will likely continue operations without much competition or governmental interference. I have personally had a good business relationship with PayPal and can endorse this service to the general public. My pricing structure automatically factors in PayPal charges that are passed along to consumers. Moreover, this business model is convenient for the buyer and seller. I believe PayPal will continue to be a

GUERILLA GARAGE SALES

viable player in the market and it will only improve on providing good service and value to consumers and businesses alike in the long term.

PART 9: INSTALLING A PAYPAL ACCOUNT

To access the PayPal website go to www.paypal.com, or the eBay homepage and click on the PayPal link under specialty sites to the left of the page. To register on PayPal you will need to disclose your personal information a second time, however, since PayPal is a subsidiary of eBay, you are getting the eBay assurance that your information will remain secure. Once you open the PayPal homepage click on *Sign up* at the top right of the page. The first decision you have to make is selecting your account type. When setting up a PayPal account, you have several options depending on the nature of your business and its size. First and foremost, you must decide whether you will accept credit card payments. If you decide not to accept credit cards then you should order a PayPal Personal Account. With this option you can send and receive money at no charge, with the option to upgrade to a PayPal Premier/Business account at any time. The downside is that you cannot receive credit card payments with this option. Thus, you are limiting your buyers' payment options, which in turn will limit your potential customers. In my experience, to reach a broader audience I have found you will need to set up a PayPal Premier/Business Account. This account allows you to accept any type of payment (including credit cards) for a reasonable fee, but still affords the features of the Personal account, including a customer service hotline and special auction/merchant tools for sellers. The only difference between the Premier and Business Accounts is that under the Business Account you can do business under a corporate or group name, rather then your personal name.

After filling out all of the information and submitting it, a test e-mail will be tendered to confirm your e-mail address, thus activating your PayPal account.

VII

NAVIGATING THE PAYPAL WEBSITE

Before you can send and receive payments on PayPal you need to become familiar with the features of the website, and get your bearings straight. The following is a brief synopsis of each area of the PayPal website. There are eight words at the top of the PayPal home page that control everything on PayPal. The three top links to the right of the page are *Sign Up/ Log In*, *Log Out*, and *Help*. The five links in the middle of the page towards the top are *Welcome, Send Money, Request Money, Merchant Tools*, and *Auction Tools*.

SIGN UP

Using this link will allow you to both register and set up an account on PayPal, an eBay company.

LOG IN / LOG OUT

Every time you need to sign into your PayPal account, you will have to use *Log In* by presenting your e-mail address and password. For security purposes, PayPal automatically encrypts your password every time you log in. Furthermore, whenever you want to leave the PayPal website, be

GUERILLA GARAGE SALES

absolutely certain to click on the *Log Out* link to keep hackers from stealing your information and logging in after your departure.

HELP

Have a question? Need an answer? This is the place to go when everything else fails. You can access the entire PayPal database for answers to all of your important questions. You can begin by clicking on PayPal's *FAQ's* (frequently asked questions) at the top of the page. If you have a specific question not covered by FAQ's, just type it in the *Search* box. After navigating these options if you are still unable to find an answer, then you can contact eBay by clicking on *Contact Us* to the left of the page. Unfortunately you will not receive an immediate response. You will receive a promised e-mail response from someone within 24-48 hours. However, if you have an issue of immediate concern then you can call the PayPal Service Center at 1-888-221-1161. For security reasons, you will be asked to provide your telephone number, e-mail address, and the last 4 digits of your credit card or bank account registered with PayPal.

WELCOME

The Welcome link acts just as the *Home link* on the eBay website. The Welcome link is a useful maneuver to take you back to the PayPal starting page from any other webpage on the PayPal website. No matter where you are, or how lost you may be, clicking on the *Welcome link* returns you to the PayPal main page.

SEND MONEY

The most repeated catch phrase from college students to their parents, this feature allows you to send payment to anyone with an e-mail address, for any reason. This is a very useful function when you send a full or partial refund to a disgruntled purchaser. The only requirement is the recipient's e-mail address and amount of money you wish to send. The money will be automatically deducted from your credit card or checking account. Furthermore, in addition to U.S. dollars, you can send money in the form of most major currencies, including Canadian Dollars, Euros, Pounds Sterling, and Yen. This is a necessity when negotiating foreign transactions.

REQUEST MONEY

Just like the Send Money feature, all you need is an e-mail address to *Request Money*. To get money, just invoice a customer by entering his e-mail address and the required amount. The e-mail will provide easy instructions to the customer to implement PayPal payments. Payments will be automatically deposited into your PayPal account.

MERCHANT TOOLS

Have you considered accepting credit card payments, but found it unaffordable? Well, with PayPal, accepting credit card payments is inexpensive and efficient. PayPal is able to offer a variety of merchant tools to fit your needs:

- ⊕ Manage PayPal payments: From here you can access your payment history for the prior year and download it into your management software (like Microsoft Excel) to handle your business activities, such as taxes.

- ⊕ Shipping and tracking tools: Here you can utilize either USPS or UPS to ship your items by printing labels and tracking numbers.

- ⊕ Invoice your customer: By using Winning Buyer Notification e-mails (WBN), PayPal will automatically send a customized e-mail invoice to your customer. This e-mail will include everything the buyer needs to respond, including the item price, shipping cost, item number, and payment options.

AUCTION TOOLS

Just like its parent company, PayPal provides a number of useful tools to help you manage your auctions and eBay listings:

- ⊕ Add PayPal logo to your auction: Let buyers know that you accept PayPal and that they have a safe and easy way to pay for your listings.

GUERILLA GARAGE SALES

- Manage eBay items sold: When you use PayPal's Post-Sale Manager you can keep track of your items that have already sold, by e-mailing the buyers, sending payment invoices, and leaving feedback.

VIII

SECOND FRONT—THE "HALF TRACK" IN COMBAT

You might be surprised to learn that the bulk of my Internet sales transactions have been conducted on *Half.com*, a huge marketplace, (*not eBay*). It is one of the most innovative sites to buy and sell quality, new, and pre-owned music, books, CD's, video games, movies, and other items at discount prices. My grandfather calls it the "no-bid equivalent of eBay." This multi-faceted business model originally promoted everything for sale at "one-half off" its original selling price. Several years after its debut, Half was acquired by eBay. After the eBay merger/acquisition, market forces primarily influenced Half's pricing structure rather than the advertised "half-off" sales stratagem; however, eBay retained the brand name "Half." Accounting for a majority of my sales revenue, initially I did not write one word about Half.com for this book because before I went to press in 2004, it was announced that plans to fully integrate Half with the eBay platform were being put on hold. To compound matters, ensuing press releases indicated that eBay intended to wind up the affairs of its subsidiary in July of 2004; when the avowed termination date arrived, eBay nonetheless extended its self-imposed deadline to October, thus avoiding a colossal tactical blunder, in my view. Thus, when the site continued to grow and thrive in spite of imminent annihilation, in October 2004, eBay had a change of heart, and announced the site's demise would be postponed indefinitely. After a complete course reversal and making uncharacteristic amends, eBay elected to scrap the closure entirely and stated it expects to continue making investments and improvements in Half.com along with its core eBay trading business. It is potentially quite significant that this company continues to be a viable selling platform. I believe sales continue to remain strong on the

GUERILLA GARAGE SALES

"Half Track" because there is a distinct buyer expectation directed toward it as opposed to other trading platforms. This business model employs "fixed prices by design" and it has a strong following that remain loyal for that reason. Habitual patrons like my father, who already know what they want, go to this site, buy, and log out. eBay shoppers like my neighbor are more auction-oriented and have a contrary shopping expectation. Without discussing the near folly of eBay in pursuing destruction of this unique company, as a frequent seller, I have found Half to be equal to the task and a superior venue to all other business models, including its parent eBay. I am one of its loyal supporters and I believe you will be also, if you sell books, games, music, and movies, and have a minimum of time.

There are some obvious reasons for its success. As a seller, you realize many tangible benefits when you utilize Half in your business arsenal—nearly all perfunctory functions required by traditional auction sites to list and sell your items are handled by the house. Preparing your inventory for sale is a breeze. Instead of hours of writing ad copy, taking and manipulating pictures, navigating templates and writing HTML, you can completely offer almost any item for sale in a minute or less. Simply type a name, ISBN or UPC number (standard commercial codes found on all products), indicate condition, and choose a price. Bam! Your item is listed! Half.com's database has a stock picture library with millions of images. If your item is included in their archives, you are immediately in business. I have found a majority of my inventory in their database, but when they are not, they are often added later. Besides images, Half also prepares a brief synopsis of the item and encapsulates basic information and features you would likely employ in the ad copy had you been drafting it yourself. When pricing goods, its format affords you an average sales price for an item as well as the last sold price, to guide you in your pricing decision. By the way, there is *NO CHARGE* to list any item on Half.com! There are *no* start-up fees, listing fees, or monthly fees. You only pay a final gross value fee of fifteen percent when the item sells. And, there are no listing deadlines or problems normally associated with re-listing an item. Once an item is offered for sale on Half, it stays on the site until purchased, or you remove it. What about dealing with customers and handling the money? Other than Feedback, occasionally customers may have questions about your products, however all correspondence is channeled indirectly through the web site and not to you, so everyone can view the product discussion. Normally no other buyer communications are needed or allowed unless there is a problem with an order, or special handling requirements. One feature I prefer is that you do not have to collect the money or concern yourself with checks clearing, money orders, or credit cards. Half.com collects the proceeds, deducts its commission, calculates shipping costs, and prepares the shipping invoice, which is immediately electronically forwarded to you with the order. Once Half transmits the order to the seller, there are no charge backs to the merchant's account unless the item is damaged, undelivered, or its condition varies from the advertised declaration in your listing. When notified by Half, you can ship right away and get your product in the hands of your customer without apprehension or delay. All you have to do is print the invoice from the site, pack, and ship. Twice a month you receive a direct deposit to your bank account for your share of the sales proceeds and shipping allowance minus Half's commission.

IX

HOW TO SELL ON HALF

Half.com is a wonderful resource to sell merchandise, without all the hassles of other behemoth websites such as Amazon and Yahoo. As a matter of fact, it is owned by eBay, so you know that it is dependable with a very user-friendly format for both sellers and buyers. Moreover, at Half.com there are no initial fees. You never pay a penny until you have sold something on the website. You even receive a free merchant account and all customer credit card payments are processed for you at no charge. There are also no charge back credit card risks! This is great place to resell you stuff! To get started go to your browser, type www.half.com into the address bar, and click *GO!*

STEP 1: BECOME A MEMBER

Becoming a Half.com user is easy. Just log onto the Half website, scroll to the bottom of the page, and click on *Register*. You can also click on *Sign In* at the top right of the page and click on *Register* to the left after the page is done loading. Perhaps one of the best advantages to having an eBay account is that this information will automatically transfer when registering on Half and you do not need to create a new account at Half.com. Instead, your eBay User ID and Password will work on Half.com. The registration process for Half.com will only take a few minutes. Once it is complete you will be able to list on both sites. You can use the same User ID and password for your Half.com account, and all your feedback from both sites will be in one feedback forum. Please remember; however, that you will be billed separately from eBay and Half.com for listing and final value fees.

STEP 2: Create a Seller's Account

If you already have a seller's account on eBay, then click on the *My Account* link at the top of the page and log into your eBay account. (Note: If you wish to create a new account just for Half, click on *My Account* and then select *Register* at the left of the page. You will have to register a new account just like you did with eBay.) Next, click on the *Start Selling Now* link towards the left of the page or at the middle of the screen. Now enter your credit card information and click *Next*. On the next page you must enter your financial information, including the name of your bank and check routing information. From now on Half will automatically deposit your payments into your bank account (which you provided). Payment periods will end on the 15th and last day of each month. It may take up to 7 days for the deposit to appear in your account. Congratulations, you are done! Now when you visit your Half account you will now have added options and features for selling functions, such as inventory management and sales histories.

STEP 3: Sell Your Stuff

Go to the Half.com home page, and click on *Sell Your Stuff* towards the top of the page. Then select the product category that your item falls under. For example, if you are selling a book click on the Books link, if it is a CD or album click on Music, and so on. Then, depending on the type of item, just type in the code number in the box (ISBN for books, product name for game systems, and UPC code for movies/DVDs, music, and video games) and click continue. (Note: You can also bypass this option and just type in the ISBN or UPC code in the Half.com Quick Sell box at the bottom of the page.)

Now it is time to provide information about your product to prospective buyers. At the top of the page, scroll and give the condition. It is extremely important that you choose an accurate condition rating regarding your items for sale. If you wish to expound upon the condition or give any other relevant information regarding the item for sale you can do so in the Comments box and Description box. Under the Comments section, you have the option of providing any additional information you feel is necessary, up to 500 characters in length. In the Description box you can enter full information about your item up to 80,000 characters. I personally go into a little more detail about item condition and expand upon product details when I list my items for sale. Also, I blow my own horn a little and give the prospective customer information regarding my sales history, including orders confirmed, successful transactions completed, and Feedback history. You might consider the same course of action. In addition to including comments about your merchandise, you can also Upload an Image (images must be GIF or JPEG files under 2MB) by clicking on the Browse button. Moreover, if you have a picture-hosting source you can include the web address under the Enter an Image URL box. However, both of these options are unnecessary most of the time because Half usually has a stored product image of most items available for sale, along with additional product information. Furthermore, unlike eBay, most buyers do not necessarily care if there is a picture of the item. Nevertheless, you may want to include one of your own pictures of an item for sale if the stored product image library Half provides is different than your item for sale. Nonetheless, it is understood that not all items listed will necessarily match Half's product images, and just to be safe, you should mention that fact in the Comments and Description sections when you list.

Now click on *Continue* and enter the item price (75 cents or more) and quantity. On this page Half includes pricing information to help you with your pricing decision. Depending on the condition rating you choose to list under (Brand New, Like New, Very Good, Good, and Acceptable). Half includes the average sale, last sold (will not be included if item has never sold before), and current price ranges for your item. Also displayed is the current price range for all categories. You need not blindly accept this information, but you should at the very least take it into consideration before making your pricing decision. Next, enter the quantity of your items for sale (up to 1,000) if you have multiple copies of one item in the same condition. Then just click on the List Item button and your merchandise will appear to millions of potential buyers within two hours.

Congratulations, you have successfully listed your first item on the Half.com website! However, this option may seem tiresome if you have many items to sell at once. In this case, click on the Multiple Item Listing link towards the bottom of the Sell Your Stuff page to list more than one item at a time. This nifty way of selling gives you the option to list ten unique items at one time. Just type in the ISBN/UPC, scroll and give the condition, add any necessary information about the item under the *notes column* and click continue. From this page, just enter the item price, give the quantity, and list.

There is one more convenient way to list your items on Half.com. Instead of clicking on the Sell Your Stuff link at the top right of the home page, just click on the category your item falls under at the top middle of the home page, such as Books. From there, just type in the ISBN, UPC, title, author, actor, director, album, or artist, depending on the item type.

GUERILLA GARAGE SALES

STEP 4: COMPLETING THE SALE

Once a buyer places an item from your inventory into his or her shopping cart and checks out, you will have completed your first sale. Half.com will then e-mail you with the following in the subject line: *You've Made a Sale – Please Ship Your Item* (Transaction Number). Included in the e-mail is the essential information about the order, such as the item specifics, item price, buyer's address, contact information, shipping method, and shipping date. In order to examine the order further, you must log into your Half account. Once you log in, click on the Sales link under the *Selling* column at the left of the page. You will then have the option to *mark as shipped, contact buyer, issue refund*, and *leave feedback*. Also, Half's shipping reimbursement will be displayed, as well as how much commission Half will earn. You will have three business days to ship the order after receiving the e-mail. If for any reason you are unable to ship the order within the allotted time, go to the Sales page as stated earlier and either use the *contact buyer* option to communicate with the buyer, or click on *issue refund* to cancel the order. Do not attempt to ship the order after three days to the buyer without permission. Any buyer can easily verify the exact date the item was shipped. Shipping the order after the third day will most likely result in late arrival and increase the risk of neutral or even negative Feedback. Once the buyer pays for his or her order, Half.com will withhold the sales proceeds and pay you based on your payment preference you chose during registration. This gives the buyer sufficient time to actually receive the order and notify you or Half of any problems concerning the transaction that may result in penalty.

STEP 5: SHIPPING CONSIDERATIONS

Sellers have the option of selecting the methods of shipping they wish to use (you chose this option when registering). If you wish to change or update your shipping preferences, you can do so by logging into your account and clicking on Seller Shipping Options under the *My Account* column at the left of the screen. Choosing your shipping methods can be arduous. You will have to ship via USPS Media Mail by default, but you may also select Expedited Shipping.

Once you sell an item on Half.com, you will receive a shipping reimbursement, or credit to defray the cost of shipping. Reimbursement rates are pre-selected by Half.com and cannot be altered. The amount of credit depends on the type (not weight) of item sold.

Item	USPS Media Mail	Expedited Method (optional based on Seller)
Hardcover Book	$2.33 for first item $0.90 each add'l item	$4.70 for the first item $2.75 each add'l item
Paperback Book	$1.94 for the first item $0.69 each add'l item	$4.70 for the first item $1.50 each add'l item
Music	$1.89 for the first item $0.65 each add'l item	$4.70 for the first item $1.50 each add'l item
VHS Movies	$1.94 for the first item $0.69 each add'l item	$4.70 for the first item $1.50 each add'l item
Audio Books	$1.94 for the first item $0.69 each add'l item	$4.70 for the first item $1.50 each add'l item
DVD Movies	$1.89 for the first item $0.65 each add'l item	$4.70 for the first item $1.50 each add'l item
Games	$1.89 for the first item $0.65 each add'l item	$4.70 for the first item $1.50 each add'l item

(Note: Half.com does not allow the Media Mail shipping method for any listing under the Game Systems category. In order to list your order under this category you will have to select either *Ground, Expedited Method,* or both.)

Although USPS Media Mail is usually the least expensive rate (First Class may be cheaper depending on the size, weight, and destination). Expedited will generally get your orders to their destinations faster. Media Mail is a special rate offered by the United States Post Office in order to promote the distribution of educational materials. Media Mail encompasses books, audiobooks, textbooks, CDs, cassettes, DVDs, videocassettes, video games, and computer software. In other words, this includes every category available on Half.com besides Game Systems. Although Media Mail is generally the most inexpensive method to ship merchandise; it also has one of the slowest arrival times—two to five weeks. Expedited shipping is faster but costs more. Expedited shipping literally means that the item is shipped with priority or primacy. However, when dealing with Half.com, *expedited* means any shipping method that is faster than Media Mail. Thus, as a seller, you can ship an item in numerous ways, such as USPS First Class, Priority Mail, UPS Ground, FedEx Home Delivery, Airborne Express Ground Delivery etc. The routing decision is up to the seller. Keep in mind however, that Half sets standard shipping rate reimbursements for both the Media Mail and Expedited Shipping methods. Further, expedited shipping usually results in more sales and exposure, especially during the holiday season when last minute gift orders are followed by last minute priority shipping. Also, during the bulk of the school year, many college and high school students order textbooks and literary works between semesters. Some procrastinate and fail to order until just before the beginning of class. During this last minute frantic search for textbooks, students will frequently require more expensive expedited shipping and may bypass your listing even if you have a better price but do not offer expedited shipping options. Nevertheless, if you offer an expedited shipping option, you will have to monitor your daily orders more carefully and examine each shipping method chosen by the buyer. If you make a mistake and ship via USPS Media Mail when the buyer paid for Expedited this can result in negative buyer relations, negative feedback, and eventually a loss of profit.

It is always your responsibility as the vendor to package and carefully ship the merchandise in a timely fashion. You will not be reimbursed for insurance or delivery confirmation by Half. Depending on the value of the item, you should consider these options when shipping, should the buyer claim he never received delivery or a loss occurs. I have had this happen to me a couple times, but luckily I either had insurance or documented proof of delivery. Always be careful and insure with care!

STEP 6: HALF.COM'S COMMISSION

Unlike its parent company, eBay, Half.com only charges one fee—a single commission at the end of the sale. On Half, the seller sets the price for each individual item, and it either sells or remains listed (as opposed to eBay where the listing duration is only a maximum 10 days before re-listing).

There is no end date for listings on Half, and the seller pays no fees unless the item sells.

For all items in any category under $50.00 Half's commission is 15% of the item price only (not shipping). The percentages then decrease by 2.5 as the item price increases by fifty dollars or more.

Selling Price + Applicable Shipping Costs	Half.Com Commission
<$50.00	15.0%
$50.01—$100.00	12.5%
$100.01—$250.00	10.0%
$250.01—$500.00	7.5%
>$500.00	5.0%

While a 15% commission may seem steep at first, consider the costs compared to eBay and other online-merchant websites. With Half, there are no listing fees, insertion fees, picture fees, or upgrade fees in which to confuse the seller. On eBay, not only do you have to pay an insertion when listing (and every time you re-list), but you are also charged a final value fee which is also a percentage of the sales price (5-10 percent depending on the final price). When compared to eBay and other online marketplaces, Half.com is the only way to go!

STEP 7: HALF.COM'S CONDITION POLICY

Item condition is judged differently on Half than eBay or other websites. When listing an item, providing the correct condition (from the pull down menu during the Half.com listing process) and an accurate description can mean the difference between Positive Feedback and repeat customers, or Negative Feedback and diminished sales. Unlike eBay, Half institutes set grading standards for the condition of your items: *Brand New*, *Like New*, *Very Good*, *Good*, and *Acceptable* (any item that falls below the requirements of *Acceptable* cannot be listed). Additionally, Half.com publishes these grading standards by product category and defines them.

GUERILLA GARAGE SALES

Item Quality – Books, CD's, Movies, Video Games

BOOKS

🎇 *Brand New* – New, unread, unused and in perfect condition with no missing or damaged pages.

🎇 *Like New*—Shiny, undamaged cover, dust jacket included for hard covers, no missing pages, all pages undamaged (no creases or tears), no underlining/highlighting of text, no damage to binding, no writing in margins (Could easily be mistaken for brand new).

🎇 *Very Good* – Doesn't look brand new but has no easily noticeable damage to the cover, dust jacket included for hard covers, no missing pages, all pages undamaged (no creases or tears), no underlining/highlighting of text, no writing in margins, very minimal identifying marks inside cover, very minimal wear and tear (You would give it to a good friend as a gift).

🎇 *Good* – Very minimal damage to the cover (no holes or tears, only minimal scuff marks), dust jacket not necessarily included, minimal wear to binding, majority of pages undamaged (minimal creases or tears), minimal pencil underlining of text, no highlighting of text, no writing in margins, no missing pages (You would use it yourself, but wouldn't necessarily give it as a gift).

🎇 *Acceptable* – Some damage to the cover but integrity still intact, binding slightly damaged but integrity still intact, possible writing in margins, possible underlining and highlighting of text, no missing pages (item beaten up a bit but it works).

🎇 *Unacceptable* – We won't sell it! Major damage (holes and/or tears) to a significant number of pages and/or cover, missing or stained pages, book cover is missing, book is not readable.

CDS, MOVIES, VIDEO GAMES

💣 *Brand New* – A brand new, unused, unopened & undamaged CD, movie or video game in perfect condition. There are no holes or cuts in the barcode or jewel case. The original packaging and all materials are included and in brand new condition.

💣 *Like New* – Item still in shrink wrap or looks as if it was just taken out of shrink wrap, no wear and tear, all facets of product are intact.

💣 *Very Good* – No damage at all to jewel case or item cover (no scuff marks, no scratching, no cracks or holes), cover art and liner notes included, VHS and DVD box included, video game instructions and box included, teeth of disk holder undamaged, minimal wear and tear to exterior of item, no skipping on CD/DVD, no fuzzy/snowy frames on VHS tape.

💣 *Good* – Minor damage to jewel case (scuffs or cracks) or item cover (scuff marks, scratching, or cracks), cover art and liner notes included for a CD, VHS and DVD box included, video game instructions included, no skipping on CD/DVD, no fuzzy/snowy frames on VHS tape.

💣 *Acceptable* – Tear or hole in VHS/DVD box, video game instructions and box not included. Promotional CD's and DVD's.

💣 *Unacceptable* – We will not sell it. No jewel box for CD, no box sleeve for VHS/DVD, skipping and fuzziness, item is not useable.

TEXTBOOKS

💣 *Brand New* – New, unread, unused and in perfect condition with no missing or damaged pages. No highlighting or writing on any pages or the cover.

💣 *Like New* – Shiny, undamaged cover, all pages undamaged (no creased, torn or missing pages), no writing/highlighting, no damage to binding (is or could easily be mistaken for brand new).

GUERILLA GARAGE SALES

💣 *Very Good* – Doesn't look brand new but has no easily noticeable damage to the cover, all pages undamaged (no creased, torn, or missing pages), minimal underlining/highlighting of text, minimal identifying marks in margins or inside cover, very minimal wear and tear.

💣 *Good* – Very minimal damage to the cove such as scuff marks or slightly bent covers, minimal wear to binding, majority of pages undamaged (minimal creases or tears), some pencil writing or highlighting of text (on less than 10% of the book's pages), no missing pages (you would use it yourself, but wouldn't necessarily give it as a gift.).

💣 *Acceptable* – Some damage to the cover such as scuff marks, stickers, or bent corners, some wear to binding (but integrity still intact), some pencil writing or highlighting of text (on less than 20% of the book's pages), no missing pages (book is beaten up a bit, but it works).

💣 *Tattered and Torn* – We won't sell it! Major damage (holes and/or tears) to a significant number of pages and/or to the cover, missing or stained pages, excessive highlighting, damage from water or other liquids, binding is broken, book cover is missing, book is not readable.

GAME SYSTEMS

💣 *Brand New* – Item still in original packaging and has all manuals, documentation, and OEM software (where applicable). No wear or tear and all facets of product flawless and intact. Item is still under warranty.

💣 *Like New* – Item still in original package OR looks as if it was just taken out of original package. Has all manuals, documentation, and OEM software. No wear, tear, all facets of product flawless and intact.

💣 *Very Good* – No damage to product, still in working condition, may show signs of light use. May not have original package but does have accompanying manuals.

Good – Shows signs of use, but still in functioning condition. May have original packaging and manuals.

Acceptable – Shows considerable use, but still works. May have original packaging or manuals.

Unacceptable – You can't sell it! Product no longer works or functions as intended.

Remember, correctly assessing and representing the quality of an item is extremely important. *Brand New* literally means brand new, and *Like New* means you could give the item as a gift to someone. In describing the condition of their merchandise, many sellers abuse their trust by inflating its quality. This is fraudulent, unfortunate, and is usually followed by negative Feedback. Even in today's cost cutting climate this is always a mistake!

Moreover, it is also important to base your price on the condition of the item. You do not want to sell a used textbook for 15% off the retail price and sell a brand new one for only 50%. Half will provide a suggested selling price in an effort to help you price your product competitively when listing.

So what can we conclude from this exactly? Do not focus on these numbers alone. Be aware of other sellers' pricing and consider all available information before you make a decision. In other words, just use rational behavior and always price the item to sell.

STEP 8: HALF'S POSITIVES

As someone who seeks to achieve results in today's rapidly accelerating business climate, you have a tremendous opportunity through Half.com to attract new customers and grow your business. By utilizing this model, you will have world class capabilities at your fingertips. First, a word on what is really good about Half:

- No PayPal fees to reduce your bottom line
- Dealing directly with customers is minimal
- Collection and disbursement of money is handled by the site
- List an item once and it stays on indefinitely
- Vendor charge backs or losses are nearly nonexistent
- No pictures to take, edit, or load

GUERILLA GARAGE SALES

- No ad preparation
- Fixed pricing, no auction format
- Faster listing, selling and shipping
- Timing not a concern because item stays listed until sold
- Money goes directly to your bank and not PayPal or anywhere else
- When you go on vacation you can temporarily remove your entire inventory and restore it when you return

STEP 9: HALF'S NEGATIVES

Getting to the heart of the matter, there are important factors that do not make the headlines, but do suggest that Half has some weaknesses. In assessing the data although not critical, the biggest downside to Half is:

- Sales are presently limited to only U.S., its territories, and Canada,
- Selling prices in certain areas may be lower than on other sites
- Advertising and promotion of Half.com by eBay is inadequate
- In many ways Half.com remains a well-kept secret
- Shipping regulation is more cumbersome than other sites
- Grading is less seller friendly
- Half.com shipping allowances are fixed and vendor reimbursement is often slightly sub-par, but you can make good money over the long term. In certain instances, Half charges a commission on shipping.

Looking beyond these factors, Half.com brings competition and choice to the marketplace. In a recent interview with the Harvard Business School, *Mike Eskew*, CEO of United Parcel Service offered his philosophy on package flow technology, a key to Half's success in modern supply and demand chains: "Commerce has changed. Commerce used to be three distinct movements, three separate flows. The first was the flow of information—the order entry process. The second movement was the flow of the goods. And the third was the money. These movements are no longer separable." For now and in the near future, there are definitely positive market signs to insure the continued success of the "Half-Track" in combat. Consider this eBay subsidiary in leading your unit in the battle ahead. Support the troops!

207

X

PHOTO INTELLIGENCE

Now that you have taken your pictures with either a digital camera or scanner, it is time to upload them to eBay. But first, let me state once more how important it is to have a picture of the item you are selling. Having a picture of the item that you are selling is crucial—it must clearly showcase your product to the buying public. The image you choose can highlight your item in its most favorable light, or detract from its merits. Using a photo to illustrate your item should clearly define what you are selling and must exactly confirm its condition.

You can either have eBay host your photo for another fee, or interpose your own web space. If you believe you do not have sufficient web space, check with your Internet Service Provider (ISP). Most ISP's allocate their customers a limited amount of space for a personal home page and storage. As a part of their service package, Earthlink allots 10 megabytes of personal space for each consumer. I am informed that AOL and other service providers have comparable web hosting programs.

Of course if you know HTML, or the Hypertext Markup Language used to publish these sites on the World Wide Web, you can fabricate your own web site. Generally the major ISP's have a Web Site Builder that is menu driven and similar to the system used to compose your eBay Ads. If your provider does not allow you space, you can always fall back on http://www.bravenet.com/signup/signup.php. This is a free service. Yahoo and several other companies have similar plans. There is no free lunch however, because so-called free sites bombard you with advertising to pay for your usage. Nevertheless, just to host pictures, this should suffice.

If you are a serious for profit business, I recommend obtaining your own domain name to be posted on a web-hosting site. It only takes minutes to activate. The rights to the name subscription can cost as little as $8 a year and up, and approximately $60 annually for up to 500 megabytes of space. That magnitude of storage will corral a lot of photos. With this feature you have the capability of generating sales independent of commercial sites, thus avoiding fees.

Once you contract and secure your space, you simply access it and upload pictures. Most often they are downloaded from your digital camera into your computer. If you do not have a digital camera, you will need a color scanner to transfer photos into your computer. At some point an adequate digital camera should be on your list of purchases. Once your images are loaded into your computer, you need to install them where they can be easily accessed by your eBay ad.

This requires a File Transfer Protocol (FTP) client program. These programs are easy to operate and readily available to be downloaded from the Internet. I have used WS_FTP. Their website is http://www.ipswitch.com/Products/WS_FTP/ and although the free version works well, the Pro is worth the minor cost you expend for the ease of use and lack of aggravation. Also, you do not have to continually reconnect. Once this program is installed with the coordinates provided by your SP or web-hosting provider, then you merely forward the image from your computer to your site to begin setting up the ad.

There is a tutorial for using this site. You may intersect the file on your PC in the left-hand window, (highlight it) and also the folder you wish to begin uploading, in the right-hand window, (open it), and click the arrow pointing to the right. If the path you type in is correct the images will emerge in your ad.

To host my own images in an eBay ad would look something like this:

```
<IMG src="http://www.my_domain_name.net/ebay/mypicture-1.jpg">
<BR>
<IMG src="http://www.my_domain_name.net/ebay/mypicture-2.jpg">
<BR>
<IMG src="http://www.my_domain_name.net/ebay/mypicture-3.jpg">
<BR>
<IMG src="http://www.my_domain_name.net/ebay/mypicture-4.jpg">
<BR>
```

<IMG src= tells the page that you are linking to a picture to be displayed on the page. "http://www.my_domain_name.net/ebay/mypicture-4.jpg"> tells the page where the image is located to display properly. Always include the quotes at the end of the URL or link address, or the end bracket.>

The <BR> at the end of the statement, tells the page to display the images on top of each other.

If I wanted a caption under my image, it would set up like this:

<IMG src="http://www.my_domain_name.net/ebaymypicture-3.jpg">

<P>View from top, showing the CPU and memory. </P>

In between the <P> and </P> is my descriptive text. </P> tells it to display the next picture.

If the image does not appear in the ad, then you have an error with the path you have entered. Common errors include dropping a quote or bracket, or misnaming an image.

For example:

<IMG src="http://www.My-domain_name.net/ebay/mypicture3.jpg">

Note the hyphen and capitalized M in the address, as well as the missing hyphen in the name of the image. The good news is most FTP providers will allow you to rename the image online. To effect this corrective procedure, adjust your path in the link and your image should come into view. If it does not, then check with your ISP to make sure that you are correctly entering the site address. The /ebay/ in my URL signifies that I have created a folder and named it ebay to upload my images, in order for me to link my ads to my web site. Once a unit of inventory is sold, and the image is no longer visible on eBay, I simply enter the FTP program, and delete them from the ebay folder.

Most of the Domain Name Registries also offer Web Hosting, and most Web Hosts also offer Domain Name registration. Once quite expensive, 500 MB of web space can now be budgeted for under $70 a year if you shop for it (try Google or another well-known search engine). 500 MB is a lot of pictures! As a leader expect only the best.

XI

CHATTER

Success, like good art, never happens without suffering. It is not entitlement; it has to be earned. Our environment, economy, changing demographics, and level of business competition often present unrelenting pressures on today's business owners. There is no question we live in a fast-paced world. Rapidly changing technology and competition affect all aspects of our lives. As an entrepreneur, once you realize the customer writes your paycheck, you will begin to understand how your communication role can help create satisfied, loyal, and repeat clientele that you need for your business to survive. When prospective customers ask questions about the merchandise, you must be truthful about the condition, but always try to put a positive spin on the situation. For example, I was recently asked if a book on tape was abridged or unabridged. Rather than saying: "Sorry, it is unabridged," I noted "the abridgement was approved by the author." When I get questions about whether or not a book covers certain topics, I do not just reply yes or no, I provide fundamental details to outline its contents beyond the scope of the question. When customers inquire about certain products I fully answer their question, but I also point out other significant characteristics and helpful features that may be unknown to the buyer, which could expedite the sale of the item. I always try to put myself in the buyer's position and elaborate details that would be important to me if I was considering a purchase of the identical commodity. To be successful, you must be proactive in your online business communication practices. This is a straightforward proposition. Transmit brief messages to the buyer in a friendly tone throughout the entire process. Never rely on the buyer to contact you first. It is your business and you must clearly demonstrate that you are in organized and responsible. This assures the purchaser that you are a professional who takes care of details. The main purpose of e-mails is to keep the buyer informed as to the progress of the sale. An uninformed buyer can become an unhappy buyer in a nanosecond. Always follow up immediately after your sale closes with e-mail or other communication to the buyer to encourage positive feedback such as: *Your item was shipped today USPS Media Mail at 8:00 a.m. Central Standard TEXAS Time! I hope you enjoy your selection. I will leave Feedback for you and I hope you will do the same. Thanks for your business, Austin.* Be certain to use the Bid Number and the description of the item as your e-mail subject title. Retain *all* e-mails pertaining to a sale until it is completed, feedback has been exchanged, or a dispute has been resolved. This is the only evidence of your transaction. Upon receipt, inform the buyer when you received his payment and make known exactly when you intend to ship his item. *Do not ship* until payment has fully cleared your account and advise the buyer in advance. Whenever problems arise always bite your tongue and turn your cheek—stay calm and friendly and continue the dialogue. This is not hypocrisy; it is TACT! You must maintain the patience and skill of a listener—you cannot *understand* your customer until you *hear* him. Being able to win the debate in this business is a much less valuable skill than being able to listen intently. Do you know what each buyer wants and needs? Do you always hear them correctly? True communication with your trading partner is more than hearing if it lacks complete understanding. When things go awry what often happens is a psychological human behavior response. When we hear or see something, all kinds of data are unconsciously transmitted to our brain. Since we are creatures of habit that require logic and order, whenever we do not receive all of the information, our brain automatically fills in the gaps. Your brain fills in the missing information with data from your experience and personality. In effect, our brain lies to us. When things get out of kilter, the brain clings to things that are comfortable and familiar to a person. This is normal human behavior and it usually helps us think and react quickly to stimulus in our lives even though we do not have all of the data. Without this type of naturally-occurring cerebral phenomena, we would continually face a reactive paralysis to even the most benign situations in our living environment before our mind could gather the additional missing information and muster a response. The problem we face in business often occurs when your customer's brain does the same thing as yours, and you both are not on the same page. The challenge is to first sort out the facts from conclusions, feelings, and fiction. The lesson to be learned is to listen before you speak and maintain the patience and skill of a listener first. In order to really listen, you must *remain silent*. Once you have all of the information in hand, go ahead, take action, and make a decision. According to *Benjamin Franklin*, the real art of communication is "not only to say the right thing in the right place, but far more difficult still, to leave unsaid the wrong thing at the tempting moment."

You should always remain in firm control of the transaction. Nonetheless, abusive e-mails that cross the line should be reported to eBay, Amazon, or other site you may be using. You can also report the abuser to their Internet Service Provider by typing "abuse@ (add their ISP provider.****)." You are the trained professional. Do not allow an angry customer to negatively impact your business. This is vital to your strategic objective. You are going to encounter non-paying bidders, called an "NPB" by eBay, and you will inevitably receive negative feedback that you do not deserve. This is always frustrating, but it is a part of business. Just accept it. Whenever you get a "NPB" follow the eBay regimen to recapture your Final Value fee and re-list the item. This process when properly followed to its final conclusion will also register a NPB against the buyer. If the offender receives two more infractions, eBay will suspend his privileges. Leave Feedback only after the customer acknowledges receipt and registers his comments regarding your merchandise and services, or you have finished the eBay Non Paying Bidder Alert process. Some buyers distort the spirit of the Feedback system and attempt to extort concessions from you with the threat of negative Feedback. You never know what a customer will register about you until he has fully revealed his hand. I have received negative Feedback after a routine transaction without a hint of problems. I rarely leave negative feedback because I feel I have too much to lose. I do not want to receive negative Feedback from some *Internut* or a NPB, who usually has little at risk. This is a calculated business decision that every businessperson needs to make, because feedback is the first line of defense to protect the public from difficult or dishonest people. When you withhold the truth out of fear of revenge, the person will likely perpetrate a similar offense on another unsuspecting *Netizen*. When I respond to negative feedback I do not attack under any circumstances. According to my attorneys you can *defame* by feedback. Defamation is another legal term you need to commit to memory. If your feedback makes a false statement or unfairly ridicules someone over the Internet you could be sued if your statements are ultimately found to be false and malicious. Published or written defamation is called *libel* and is legally actionable. Whatever you say in your feedback is published to millions of eBay users and it cannot be retracted. If you are wrong or ill advised, the damages could be substantial. Just because you only sell on the Net part time or are ignorant of the law is no excuse. You are competing in a commercial arena opposite Special Forces and trained mercenaries and are equally liable for your actions. Of course truth is an absolute defense, but if you have to pay your legal counsel $350.00 an hour to defend you in court you are going to lose the battle even if you win the war, because lawsuits seemingly last forever when you are the defendant. "Ignorance of the law must not prevent the losing lawyer from collecting his fee"—*John Mortimer.* Because you own the company does not influence the defense of your lawsuit, and your personal views will have little impact on the final outcome. You lose control to lawyers, the judge, a mediator, and other legal personnel. Can you comprehend the impact of thousands of dollars worth of billable hours stemming from a lawsuit against you, not mention its effect on your business? This is what you will likely pay a law firm to represent you in and out of court, even if you are technically innocent. Legal fees can be so astronomical that one lawsuit can put you out of business. You can never foresee false accusations being made against you. Therefore, before you publish anything on the Internet, always ask yourself in advance: what statement am I making; what do I gain from this communication, am I enhancing or detracting from my mission?

I always try to leave Feedback even though roughly 40% of purchasers I encounter fail to return the favor. Therefore, I purposely leave appropriate feedback that is not misleading or too uncomplimentary. I merely accept blame if I made a mistake, or briefly outline why the perceived problem was not my fault. I also focus on my overwhelming performance history of good feedback and total of successful sales transactions to date. Responding and leaving Feedback in these instances is difficult because eBay allows you a single opportunity with only 80 characters to craft an answer. This is a daunting task if you endeavor to rebut the charges and publish your overall business record within the meager space you are permitted to respond.

Once Feedback is posted it cannot be removed except in certain limited instances:

✠ "eBay is provided with a ruling or settlement agreement from an eBay-approved certified dispute resolution service. Such a ruling may be

GUERILLA GARAGE SALES

issued if the feedback recipient initiated a dispute resolution process and the member who left the feedback does not respond to the request for mediation.

✠　eBay is provided with a valid court order finding that the disputed feedback is slanderous, libelous, defamatory or otherwise illegal, or with a settlement agreement resolving such a lawsuit submitted by both attorneys and signed by both parties.

✠　The feedback, on its face, has absolutely no connection with eBay, such as feedback related to commercial transactions that were not conducted through eBay. This also includes feedback that contains any reference to another auction service or feedback that advertises the goods or services of someone other than the user for whom the feedback was left.

✠　The feedback contains any link to another page, picture, or JavaScript.

✠　The feedback contains profane or vulgar language, or adult material. Inflammatory language, such as "fraud, liar, cheater, scam artist, con man" etc. is strongly discouraged but will not be removed.

✠　Feedback that contains personal identifying information about another user, including real name, address, phone number, or e-mail address.

✠　Feedback that makes any reference to an eBay or law enforcement organization investigation, i.e., "eBay is investigating this person".

✠　Negative feedback intended for another user will be considered for removal only in situations where the user responsible for the mistaken posting informs eBay of the error and has already placed the same feedback for the correct user. This does not apply to a comment that was mistakenly marked negative instead of positive or vice versa.

✠　Feedback left by a user who provided eBay with false contact information during the transaction period (as verified by eBay), and cannot be contacted.

✠ Participating in an eBay transaction with the intent of leaving feedback as part of a campaign to harass one or more members.

✠ eBay may give special consideration to remove feedback upon request from members if the listing ended before the member was suspended, but the feedback was left after we reinstated the member."

Besides providing a forum for positive Feedback, negative Feedback, or no Feedback, eBay has a neutral feedback category. Feedback is a paperless trail of your online reputation. It is a rating system that publishes to the world a user's overall business history, including such tangibles as the quality of goods, customer communication, payment history, service, and shipping. Feedback is also a comment left by a registered user about their buying, selling, or trading experiences with another user. After each sale both parties to a transaction have an opportunity to rate their counterpart's business practices. Positive feedback is one point and negative feedback is minus one point. No points are awarded for neutral feedback or when no feedback is left. Since almost half of my transactions are not rated by Feedback, I publish my total completed sales figures in my ads (over 8,500 to date) and correspondence, in order for my customers to know how many actual transactions I have handled. I believe that everyone should leave some form of feedback after each transaction but I am barely in the majority on this point. When a transaction is clearly substandard, negative feedback is an obvious choice. When things are not quite up to par or so-so I consider leaving a neutral posting. Poor communication skills, product quality deficiencies, and shipping problems clearly at the feet of the other party might warrant a neutral feedback rating. Although not a prerequisite, as a common courtesy I usually give my trading partner an opportunity to do the right thing before I post a neutral or negative comment. Quite often differences can be rectified amicably and both parties leave each other a positive rating at the conclusion of the sale. *Shakespeare* said it best: "All's well that ends well."

Always remember: to get ahead, you must develop a reputation for honesty and build a stable of favorable feedback comments from your buyers. Furthermore, everything from you conveys an image about your business that affects the customer's perception about you. The case can be easily made that within one click of your operation there are numerous competitors eager and capable of doing business with your customers. It takes a long time to develop a good reputation. Just a few negative comments can ruin your business in an instant. A few bad comments can destroy everything you have accomplished and require a very long time to recoup. This can be illustrated by comparing one seller who has a low Feedback number and three negatives in the past month—with a second seller having a considerable selling history, no negatives, and a 100% Feedback rating. If you were a buyer which seller would you choose? A low feedback number generally indicates a new account. This could be someone new to eBay, or an individual that was punished for his selling or buying practices, now operating under a new name and identity. I am aware the stigma of bad feedback can be awarded unjustly, but out of an abundance of caution the free market makes a clear distinction in matters like this. Avoid being in this predicament and stay away from those who are.

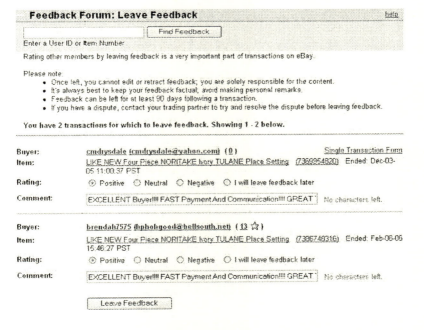

Moreover, eBay also graphically communicates your current Feedback scores to the public in every sales listing on their site, by prominently displaying an appropriate colored star in the body of each seller's ad and a corresponding star by the name of each bidder. There are various colored stars and each one is a milestone that represents attainment of one's ever-increasing feedback score. The star rating system begins after a new applicant's initiation period of 10 transactions marked by a yellow star that indicates a feedback rating between 10 and 49 points. This is accompanied by a blue star of 50 to 99 points, then turquoise, which represents 100 to 499 points, and so on—up to a red shooting star which indicates a feedback score of 100,000 points or higher.

Finally, eBay does not allow you to create direct links, or URL links to your own site or any third party. However, there is a way to create "legal" links that will enable one to access these sites. You can achieve this by placing additional photos on your auction site; then use a link from your site to these photos. Thus, you are able to attract people from the photos to visit your site. Keep in mind that you can also create links from your logo. But once again, eBay does not allow a text URL link on the page directly to your site. However, you can provide URL links if they are in relation to eBay. For example, I always provide a link in my auctions directing prospective buyers to a page with all of my other eBay listings going on at the same time. To do this, you must use the following URL link and enter your eBay user ID:

http://cgi6.ebay.com/ws/eBayISAPI.dll?ViewSellersOtherItems&userid= enteruseridhere&include=0&since=-1&sort=3&rows=50

Additionally, you can also include a link to your e-mail account by entering the following text, along with your e-mail address: mailto:enteryouremailaddresshere Furthermore, you can also provide a link to other eBay mediums such as PayPal or Half.com. To do this for PayPal enter the following text: https://www.paypal.com

To do this for Half.com enter the following text and you Half.com user ID: http://stores.half.com/enteruseridhere. Keep in mind that eBay will provide these links for you, but I always them just in case, and they make my ads look better than before.

The competitive, frenetic business world and information environment in which we now live has already altered many aspects of our lives, either directly or indirectly. With the click of a computer mouse, the Web's global presence creates some potentially complicated legal issues for e-retailers as well as opening new avenues for information retrieval, commerce, and other activities at millions of web sites. By operating in a global environment today, e-retailers face potential exposure to laws governing business activities, but they also have the greatest opportunity in history to satisfy their

GUERILLA GARAGE SALES

own specific interests and needs. The good thing about online selling is, with feedback you know how good you are or how bad every day. There's power in that.

XII

SAFE HARBOR

God has created a perilous world and mankind has only made it more hazardous. During the Second World War the French Underground had a saying: *When in danger go to the heart of it, for there is where you will find safety.* Almost sixty years ago during the height of the German occupation of Europe, resistance fighters kept their enemies close to them and their friends at a distance. The underground often remained safe because the enemy never expected to find organized opposition hiding under its very nose. The cold reality was the resistance could not befriend or trust anyone—their very lives depended on it. Today we are mostly a society of warriors without armed conflict, but we must not fool ourselves; we are at war. We lived in an age of keeping to ourselves, but the Internet changed that brief isolation forever. At this very moment millions of items are for sale online. There are hundreds of thousands of individuals around the world who are making a good living selling on the Internet to millions of potential buyers who are constantly surfing the Web. Truthfully, the Internet can be a great selling tool but it is also a prime scamming resort for those on the opposite side of the law. How else in June of 2005 could VISA and MASTERCARD allow criminals to appropriate 40 million credit card numbers from their system? A prime objective of Guerilla Garage Sales is for the reader to be forewarned, so that he can be forearmed. If this serious security breach can happen to professionals like VISA and MASTERCARD, no one is completely safe. According to experts, statistics consistently support the fact that one of every four computers in the USA is infected with some type of virus and even larger numbers have no spyware programs. This enables an uninvited third party to have access to your computer files. Some covert programs can record every keystroke you make without your knowledge. Fortunately, no victim of a computer virus has died yet, but until the Justice department starts levying real sentences for these individuals, and refrains from prosecuting them as juvenile pranks and childish mischief, this problem will likely continue unabated. Regardless, we all have to be vigilant and protect ourselves the best way we can. In over five years of selling on the Internet, I have never been scammed. As a seller I am confident there is almost no reason for being cheated if you follow the rules and take reasonable precaution.

According to the Federal Trade Commission, "over 635,000 complaints [were reported] during the calendar year 2004—61% represented fraud and 39% were identity theft complaints." As a result, "consumers reported fraud losses of over $547 million and the percentage of complaints about *Electronic Fund Transfer* related identity theft more than doubled between 2002 and 2004." The National Fraud Information Center, a branch of the National Consumers League, reported in the same year that Internet Auctions contributed to 51% of the bulk of Internet scams, phising was 5%, Fake Checks were 3%, and Fake Escrow Services were 1% of all reported scams. Finally, the NCL categorized the top five fraudulent payment methods: Credit Cards led the way with 29%, followed by Money Orders with 21%, Bank Debit accounted for 12%, Debit Cards and Checks each added 9% to the total. Use great care in dealing with others who contact you to purchase your products outside of eBay or any other commercial platform. The person prevailing upon you to skirt the rules may not be entirely honest. And, you can lose your selling privileges if this fact becomes known to eBay as well as many other websites. In the above hypothetical instance, if a person is dishonest with larceny on his mind, you will also have no recourse through your selling platform to recoup your losses or advise others of this treachery. Selling through eBay may look complicated to the uninitiated. It may seem like traveling a mile of expressway with a dozen tollbooths between you and the exit, but you are afforded some meaningful recourse in making a non-paying bidder unwelcome, or coercing a non-conforming seller to refund your money. When it comes to the rules of eBay there are no grays; the black and whites take over. eBay does make a concerted effort to protect you and your identity and to make your buying experience safe. Do not rest on your laurels, however. It is a jungle out there. Make it a routine practice to change your passwords—and get a good anti-virus, and anti-spam software removal program. A good free of charge anti-virus program is AVG from www.grisoft.com and the spyware detector I use is *Spybot Search and Destroy*, from http://www.spybot.info/en/index.html, which does not cost anything. *Ad Aware* is another complimentary program from Lavasoft. This program and Spybot have some conflicts that need to be addressed however. If your ISP has a spam blocker, and virus checking for your e-mail, be sure it is enabled. Once again, I cannot over-emphasize the virus, spyware, and password precautions. Keep updates current by scanning your computer files at least once a week. Sometimes Internet business is more virtual than real.

PLAYING IT SAFE ON EBAY

As a seller, whenever you participate in any Internet transaction you are frequently exposed to some risk. Unfortunately, the clicking of your mouse could also be the sound of counterfeit monies, hot checks, bad credit, untrustworthy buyers, fraud, and other scams being perpetrated against you. First, be aware of the threat and then take steps avoid personal exposure to these hazards. With vigilance, you can eliminate most unpleasant encounters on the Web and ensure that your selling experience on eBay is safe, pleasant, and rewarding. I recommend following safety guidelines for navigating the eBay website:

Review all potential buyers' Feedback—during the auction you should always analyze potential bidder/buyer Feedback by clicking on their user ID. If you are selling in the auction format and find that you are not comfortable with a particular eBay user because of their Feedback rating, you have the option to cancel their bid and block them from bidding on your items in the future. The reverse is also true when the buyer retracts its bid for the same reason.

Offer tracking numbers and insurance when shipping—seriously consider these two options whenever you ship higher priced or breakable goods. This is an inexpensive way to easily resolve disputes when a buyer claims an item is broken or was never delivered.

Keep good records—maintain all shipping records to verify delivery and assist in tracking. Also, retain and store all insurance forms, custom declarations, and other documents as proof of sale and post-sale review.

ADVICE FROM EBAY

eBay makes a concerted effort to work closely with both sellers and buyers to produce a safe trading environment. In order to keep its commitment, eBay offers several tools and guidelines for sellers to help protect against fraud. These can all be found under the Help section on the eBay home page, under Protection on eBay:

Only complete transactions with the winning bidder or fixed price buyer after the completion of the eBay listing. A word of caution: never engage in a transaction outside of eBay. These "off-site sales" are not eligible for eBay services, such as Feedback and contact information requests. Also, you are responsible for getting paid and handling the transaction yourself. If the buyer is deceitful, there is no satisfactory recourse.

Review the member's contact information and verify that the information corresponds with the shipping address provided by the buyer. Once the buyer has paid for your item, you can click on its user ID to determine shipping addresses and other personal information. This basic information must match the address the buyer supplies when paying for the item.

Review the payment policies of the service platform being used to determine whether or not fraud protection is provided to sellers. This is absolutely critical and why I routinely offer PayPal as the primary payment option in my online listings. The PayPal brand is respected, trusted, and recognized by buyers and sellers all over the world. Also, it is a part of eBay and I am confident that I can utilize the service with little trepidation. For high dollar transactions you may consider an escrow service, but this type of service is not recommended for transaction under $500 because the fees are prohibitive. eBay recommends the www.escrow.com, site but there are also several other websites that can be accessed for this purpose.

In the event the buyer sends fraudulent payment, contact law enforcement in your area and authorities where the buyer resides. eBay states it will "fully cooperate with all law enforcement inquiries." If for example, any payment is reversed, stopped, or cannot be received, it is your responsibility to contact the payment issuer (whether it be the credit card company, issuing bank, PayPal, etc.) to review options available to you. In other words, you must take responsibility and not simply rely on others to rectify your problem or protect your interests.

BUYER NEVER PAID

If you shipped an item and have been unable to receive or claim payment, you have the right to start the eBay *Unpaid Item* process (within 45 days, but not before 7 days after the transaction date) in order to get your *Final Value Fee* refunded. To do this, log into eBay, click on My eBay and go to the Items

I'm Selling page. Next, click on the Dispute Console at left of the page in the middle of the column. (Note: for a faster way to begin the *Unpaid Item* process, click on Community at the top of any eBay page, scroll down to *Marketplace Safety*, and click on Security & Resolution Center). Then follow the directions and links provided. First, eBay will send out a friendly e-mail reminding the buyer to pay for the item. If the buyer is steadfast in its refusal not to pay or does not contact the seller, then the seller may file for a *Final Value Fee* credit (that takes 10 days to receive after the complaint filing). After the complaint filing you are then free to re-list your item for sale. However, you may want to first consider the *Second Chance Option* to notify other bidders that the item is still available, and that the sale was not consummated. For example if your Noritake china went to the highest bidder for $89.00 but the buyer withdrew or is unable to pay, you can send out a special customized e-mail via eBay to inform the second highest bidder (who bid $75.00 for example) that the item was not sold. Should the second highest bidder fail to accept this offer, then you can e-mail other lesser bidders in descending order until the offer is accepted, or you exhaust the bidding pool. There are no extra charges for the *Second Chance Auction* service, but final acceptance of any offer will trigger the standard auction final value fees.

Accessing the *Unpaid Item* process option and filing for your final value fees will also begin the process to remove a nonconforming buyer from eBay. Three complaints from separate sellers will ultimately label the bidder NARU (Not A Registered User) and automatically result in their forced removal from the site. Furthermore, a NARU cannot post Feedback; therefore there should be little fear of bogus or retaliatory Feedback responses from this type of trading partner.

MY ACCOUNT IS HIJACKED

When you sign in and log into my eBay, if an unknown person is using your account to bid, leave Feedback, or especially to list items without your permission, then your account is under siege. The following protocol should be followed if you suspect an unauthorized party has accessed or has attempted to access your eBay account:

Attempt to sign in and change your password—try logging into your eBay account. If you are able to sign in, go to my eBay and click on Personal Information under *My Account* in the left hand column of the page. Review and edit all of your information, including passwords, addresses, and financial information. Next, begin to undo any damage done by the hacker, such as removing any bogus auctions, contact bidders and sellers, and so on. Whether or not you are able to regain control of your account, take these remaining steps!

Contact eBay—eBay has just set up a new link for *Hijacked Accounts*. To access this link, click on Help at the top of any eBay page, then click on Transaction Problems at the bottom of the page, next click Protection for Sellers, and enter into Reporting Account Theft. If that link is not available, access the Live Help button on the main eBay homepage. Some people manage to get excellent, immediate help at this location, while others are merely told to use the *Help Form*. If you get the latter response, continue to try again until you get a live helper. If Live Help is not available or not helpful, go to Help at the top of any eBay page, and click on Contact Us toward the left side. Select *Report fake eBay e-mails (spoofs) and unauthorized account activity*, then click on *Unauthorized account activity (account security issues)*…and whichever option is most appropriate. Press Continue and follow the links and advice provided by eBay, or send an e-mail.

Install and/or update AntiVirus and Firewall software—some hackings are the result of virus attacks and/or Trojans being inserted into your computer. Update all virus definitions, run a full scan, and confirm every connection your firewall allows. If your system appears to have been compromised, fix it and then change your password again, since you likely transmitted the new one to the hacker.

Check other personal accounts for fraud—the hacker may have helped himself to more than just your eBay account. Check PayPal, Half.com, your e-mail account, banking institutions, credit card services, and everything else you use online passwords to access. There is no good reason to delay in changing all your passwords *immediately*. In addition to looking for any obvious account changes, make sure no new sub-accounts were added to PayPal or your e-mail. If any of these have been altered in any way, contact the appropriate customer service center as soon as possible.

If unable to regain account control—eBay will likely suspend the account until they complete their investigation. This may take days, weeks or even a month, and there may be minimal communication during that time. Even if you successfully wrestle back your account from the brink, you may need to contact *eBay Billing* if any auctions were listed by the scammer, in order to receive any credits or refunds you may be due.

Protect against future attacks—some hijackers do not completely steal the victim's e-mail or eBay accounts, but prefer instead to *share* them. They often change e-mail and/or eBay settings so you no longer receive e-mail notifications regarding auction listings and end of auction confirmations. Then they post their listings along side yours. To help prevent this from occurring, check your listings and accounts regularly, and investigate anything that looks out of line.

SAFETY FIRST ON PAYPAL

Security is of critical importance to PayPal, as it should be with any online banking institution. The PayPal website advertises that its technology "evaluates transactions according to hundreds of variables in order to pinpoint potentially fraudulent activity." Moreover, it uses "unique, patent-pending methods for bank account verification [that] provide PayPal members an additional level of security, which lowers risk and increases trust for the entire PayPal community." In addition, PayPal and eBay have over 1,000 people worldwide dedicated to keeping PayPal accounts safe, and impede online criminals.

UNAUTHORIZED ACCOUNT ACTIVITY

If you ever notice an unauthorized transaction on your PayPal account, report it to PayPal immediately using the *Unauthorized Account Activity Form*. To do this, go to the PayPal homepage, click on the Security Center link at the bottom, and then click on Unauthorized Transaction at the right side of the page under the *Report a Problem* column. If you ever notice an unauthorized transaction applied to your PayPal Debit Card, report it to the card issuer by using the telephone number or e-mail address listed on the back of your debit card.

HELPING OUT THE SELLER

PayPal protects sellers from possible fraudulent payment activity by actively screening transactions for fraudulent buyers and false buyer claims, by providing a team of chargeback specialists and a resolution center to assist sellers resolve disputes in a fair manner. However, perhaps the best way PayPal protects sellers is through the *Seller Protection Policy*, which encourages good selling practices and insulate sellers from possible fraud. In case of chargeback or false claims of non-receipt, sellers in the United States, United Kingdom, and Canada are eligible to receive up to $5,000.00 USD annual coverage under the Seller Protection Policy. PayPal policy dictates that in order for a transaction to be eligible for protection under this category, the transaction must be marked as "SPP eligible and sellers must meet the following requirements:

- Have a qualified Verified Business or Premier Account
- Ship to the confirmed address on the Transaction Details page
- Retain reasonable proof of postage that can be tracked online
- Require signature receipt on items equal to or more in value than $250.00 USD

SHIPPING TO AN UNCONFIRMED ADDRESS

A confirmed address as defined by PayPal is "an address that has been reviewed by PayPal and found to be safe, based on information related to the address." Sellers can use confirmed addresses to help make informed decisions when transacting business and shipping goods. Nevertheless, while sellers can be more confident in shipping goods to a confirmed address, they can still ship to an unconfirmed address. An address remains unconfirmed because PayPal has not yet verified the information necessary for confirmation. The main problem with shipping to an unconfirmed address is that it lacks coverage under the Seller Protection Policy. Personally, I do not get too concerned about whether the buyer's address is confirmed or unconfirmed, if the value of the transaction is less than $100.00.

FAKE E-MAILS AND WEBSITES

Some eBay members are receiving false/fraudulent e-mails appearing to come from eBay, PayPal, and other commercial locations. These e-mails are known as "spoof" or "phising" e-mails and are a fraudulent attempt to harvest your private information for nefarious purposes. Bogus e-mails like these have become very commonplace, and are certainly the method of choice of the dishonest in many account hijackings. A common scenario is when a very official, genuine-looking e-mail warns that the eBay account is subject to suspension unless the recipient immediately clicks on the e-mail link provided to update their Contact Info.

Dear eBay Member,

We regret to inform you that your eBay account could be suspended if you don't re-update your account information.
To resolve this problem please visit link below and re-enter your account information:

https://signin.ebay.com/ws/eBayISAPI.dll?SignIn&sid=verify&co_partnerId=2&siteid=0

If your problems could not be resolved your account will be suspended for a period of 24 hours, after this period your account will be terminated.

For the User Agreement, Section 9, we may immediately issue a warning, temporarily suspend, indefinitely suspend or terminate your membership and refuse to provide our services to you if we believe that your actions may cause financial loss or legal liability for you, our users or us. We may also take these actions if we are unable to verify or authenticate any information you provide to us.

Due to the suspension of this account, please be advised you are prohibited from using eBay in any way. This includes the registering of a new account. Please note that this suspension does not relieve you of your agreed-upon obligation to pay any fees you may owe to eBay.

Regards,
Safeharbor Department eBay, Inc
The eBay team
This is an automatic message, please do not reply

Copyright © 1995-2005 eBay Inc. All Rights Reserved.

Another ploy being perpetrated is a scare tactic to fool someone into believing another person has appropriated their identity and account. The target of the attack is provided a link that opens to a page that looks just like eBay, with all the familiar graphics and format, but in reality it is a phony site orchestrated to steal your personal information. A recent bogus encounter goes one step further and appeals to the ego: "Congratulations! Join the eBay Silver PowerSeller Program. Come and join us. When you join the PowerSeller program, you'll be able to receive more of the support you'll need for continued success. So, why wait? Join now!"

Just how do you know if the e-mail is really from eBay or a scam? The first clue that it may be less than genuine is poor grammar or spelling. This often results from a sloppy English translation by a foreign national *Dot.Con* who usually operates offshore with impunity. But the biggest giveaway is that eBay, Half.com, and PayPal will *never* ask you for sensitive information such as passwords, bank account or credit card numbers, Personal Identification Numbers (PINs), or Social Security Numbers in an e-mail. If someone's Contact Information or Credit Card Expiration really does have a problem, a legitimate eBay e-mail will explain how to start at My eBay to update the information; no legitimate concern will ever provide an e-mail link to a web form. Additionally, those familiar with headers and hidden links will quickly spot the fact that the above e-mail originated somewhere else, and the link points to somewhere other than eBay.

If you do get a suspicious e-mail, forward it with headers to the appropriate site—spoof@ebay.com or spoof@paypal.com immediately. Do not respond to it or click any of the links. Do not remove the original subject line or change the e-mail in any way when you forward it. Make sure your e-mail begins with "fwd:" and that any hidden links are exposed. eBay considers this activity a serious breach. The spoof e-mail address currently gets a rapid response. eBay will take action to get the bogus websites and e-mail addresses shut down ASAP. Your quick action may be able to stop an innocent person from undergoing an account hijacking or identity theft.

Unfortunately if you are ever a victim of a bogus form or a spoof e-mail you may have to work hard to extricate yourself. First, log into your eBay and PayPal accounts to ascertain if any suspicious activity has occurred in your account (particularly your *Selling* account). Next, take immediate action to protect your identity and all of your online accounts. Begin by changing every password that you have used (including password hints). Check all your online accounts for any tampering, along with secondary accounts. Some of these web forms are very sophisticated. Often the threat goes far beyond passwords. They can gain access to banking information, PIN numbers, Social Security Numbers, and whatever else the criminal mind can conjure. If you have mistakenly provided banking information to an authorized third party, contact your financial institution immediately to determine whether or not your account should be closed. Most assuredly, if you have opened or clicked on a link from a spoof e-mail, waste no time in assessing whether or not a virus, worm, or other harmful techno-mayhem has been implanted in your computer. Update your antivirus software definitions at once, run a full virus scan, and refresh your firewall. When the dust settles, you may also consider downloading spyware/adware programs to deter future attacks.

As if all of this was not enough, these cyber-criminals also develop web pages that impersonate websites such as eBay, PayPal, and Half.com. These fake websites (also called "spoof" websites) try to imitate these popular sites

CASH HOFFMAN

in order to obtain your password and access your account. Before signing into any website, always check the Web address in your browser. If you click on a link in an e-mail, verify that the Web address in your browser is the same as the address shown in the e-mail. The Web address of eBay sign-in pages begins with http://signin.ebay.com/. Never type your eBay User ID and password into a Web page that does not have "ebay.com" immediately before the first forward slash (/). International eBay websites will have slightly different sign-in addresses. A complete list of sign-in pages for International eBay websites is provided below:

Site Sign-In/Login URL

Australia	http://signin.ebay.au/...
Austria, Germany, Switzerland	http://signin.ebay.de/...
Belgium	http://signin.benl.ebay.be/...
	http://signin.befr.ebay.be/...
Canada	http://signin.ebay.ca/...
France	http://signin.ebay.fr/...
Ireland, Sweden, United Kingdom	http://signin.ebay.co.uk/...
Italy	http://signin.ebay.it/...
Netherlands	http://signin.ebay.nl/...
New Zealand, Singapore	http://signin.ebay.com/...
Spain	http://signin.es.ebay.com/...
Taiwan	http://signin.tw.ebay.com/...
	https://scgi.tw.ebay.com/...

TAKE ACTION

In spite of these phising e-mails, spoof website, and other cyber-crimes, there are ways to protect yourself and your computer. Download and update your anti-virus and firewall programs religiously. Also, routinely download spyware/adware programs for added protection. You can never be too safe or have too much positive Feedback. eBay has provided a nifty tool to help protect its authorized users deter such attack. It is called the *eBay Toolbar* (for Internet Explorer users only), and utilizes a feature called *Account Guard* to help ensure you are on eBay or PayPal when you click on the intended site. To access this free service, go to any eBay web page and click on the Services link at the top of the page. Scroll down under *General Services* to the *Tools*

230

GUERILLA GARAGE SALES

row, and select eBay Toolbar. This is custom-made for the unwary or anyone who needs this security to avoid the slings and arrows of outrageous scammers who try to live off the fortunes of others.

Finally the best advice is to research and explore the eBay website and its subsidiaries. eBay has a comprehensive, yet easy to navigate library full of information and resources under the Help section, which is found at the top of any eBay web page. I also advise you to explore the Security Center at the bottom of any eBay page and the Discussion Boards found under the Community section at the top of any page. PayPal also has excellent resources for questions and research under the Help link at the top right hand side of any page. Moreover, just like its parent company eBay, PayPal has a Security Center link at the bottom of any PayPal web page, containing answers to many questions, and provides a contact method.

Admittedly, following all of the advice found in the eBay and PayPal help sections may not fully protect you from every tortuous assault or cyber-attack, but it does provide a ready source of valuable information for self protection should something untoward ever occur. The Internet can be a scary place but only if you naively allow yourself to be unprotected. With proper precaution and regular defensive maintenance, you can protect your domain, enjoy the Internet, and make a good living at the same time. And don't forget if it seems too good to be true...you know the rest. The world is filled with perilous encounters and new opportunities. Do not be deterred from your mission.

XIII

STRATEGIC WILD CARD

Okay, soldier, you are definitely officer material. You are a specialist with distinct abilities and capabilities. This is the New Millennium. The future holds bold challenges. Given the unflagging battle ahead, there will always be setbacks when you undertake a daring mission. Guerilla Garage Sales is an ongoing process. No one said it was going to be easy, but you now understand there are many things one can do to make it easier. The following fundamentals should be the motto of every soldier. Know your weapons and be able to use them proficiently. Always have your weapons ready for use. Use your weapons sparingly and only when you are reasonably certain of hitting your target. Now go out and develop your own rules of engagement. You know the only one you can count on is you. The purpose of this book is not to make you an expert weekend warrior; no book can do that. To become a battle-hardened tactical guerilla specialist you have to acquire hands-on experience by putting in long hours of tireless work, face challenges, and become more knowledgeable through constant training. It will take smarts and hard work to succeed. Those who are the best prepared will thrive. However, the most important thing to remember is that to succeed in this quasi, paramilitary undertaking, you do not necessarily have to be an expert—you just have to be reasonably good at a number of tasks. Those who are fearless are the ones who will lead. In the end you can become the leader who will make the future better. You have the ammunition you need, the decisions to make, and the resources to develop. You are an ordinary soldier living during extraordinary times. Go out and make your unit proud. And always remember there are no bad soldiers, only bad officers. Carry on!

XIV

GLOSSARY OF TERMS

ABSOLUTE AUCTION auction format where the property is sold to the highest qualified bidder with no limiting conditions or amount. *(Note: the seller may not bid personally or through an agent. Also known as an auction without reserve).*

ARMY SURPLUS goods, equipment, and material of non-strategic value sold to the public when no longer needed by the military *(a/k/a Military Surplus)*

AMMO CAN empty metal container used to store ammunition and ordinance

ARSENAL a place to store, repair, receipt, and issue weapons and ammunition

AS IS short for *AS IS WHERE IS AND WITH ALL FAULTS*; selling an item without warranties regarding its condition and fitness for a particular use *(Note: this designation should serve as warning sign to a potential purchaser that a product may be flawed, damaged, broken or less valuable, and no return privileges will be entertained by the seller).*

AS THE CROW FLIES the most direct route between two points

ASSESSMENT analyses of the security, effectiveness, and potential of intelligence activity

233

BARNACLE unadvertised garage sale in the forward area that could disrupt mission deployment

BARRACKS housing for non-married enlisted personnel

BASE OF OPERATIONS the location where most important functions are concentrated

BID CUTTING a bid at a traditional auction that is higher than the preceding bid but less than the amount of the normal bidding increment *(Note: a procedure generally only allowed once by the auctioneer to set a bid limit since this practice interferes with prescribed bidding pattern)*

BIVOUAC a temporary encampment

BLIP visible spot on radar or sonar screen indicating the number and present location of enemy aircraft, ships, or incoming ordinance

BOOT CAMP the process and facility where military recruits are trained

BRADLEY FIGHTING VEHICLE named after a World War II general, this is a modern armored personnel carrier with band tracks, crew of three, six-man infantry squad, and heavy armament

BRIEFING orally presented summary of current situation

BUYER'S PREMIUM flat fee added to the winning bid at a traditional auction paid by the buyer to cover auction house expenses.

BUY IT NOW option on eBay sales site allowing Seller to list item for a fixed price within an auction format

CACHE source of subsistence and supplies to support operations

CADRE nucleus of key personnel and equipment

CAMOUFLAGE visual disguise to blend in with surroundings

GUERILLA GARAGE SALES

CARPE DIEM term adopted by the U. S. Marine Corps; Latin translation: *"Seize the day!"*

CAVEAT a warning; a note of caution; Latin for "let him beware."

CO commanding officer

COLOSSUS the world's first programmable electronic computer invented during World War II to decipher enemy codes

COMBAT READINESS the ability to deploy and perform a planned mission at any time and under any circumstances

COMBINED SHIPPING when simultaneous winner of multiple sales items and delivery is to a single address the buyer may receive a reduced price for one delivery instead of paying the *"combined shipping"* costs

COMMAND AND CONTROL the ability of a commander to freely exercise authority over his forces in accomplishment of a mission without disruption from the enemy

COMMAND INFORMATION information provided to soldiers by their commanders to help them understand their role within their unit and their branch of service

COMMANDO a raiding style of military operation living off the land behind enemy lines performed by an elite light infantry Special Forces unit

COMMUNICATIONS ARRAY message center; transmitting, and receiving facilities

CONSIGNMENT arrangement whereby merchandise owned by one party (the seller) is sold by another party (the middleman) for a fee, usually on a commission basis

DEFAMATION that which tends to injure a persons reputation; false accusation of an offense or a malicious misrepresentation of someone's words or actions (*Note: Defamation" is the generally-used term to describe two types of conduct and does not distinguish between "libel" and "slander". Written or oral statements made by one person to another, and made public ("published"), which tend to bring the character or reputation of that person into disrepute, or to expose them to unreasonable personal embarrassment. Defamation is called "libel" if it is printed and "slander" if it is oral. Truth is an absolute defense to defamation, and under some circumstances even untruths may be privileged and immune from liability if it cannot be shown the defamation was intentional or malicious*).

DELIVERY CONTRACT seller is responsible for getting the item to the purchaser and bears the risk of loss for damage occurring to goods after the sale has been completed but before delivery has occurred (*Note: the seller chooses the shipping method, manner, and carrier. If something goes wrong, the carrier is his agent and he has to indemnify the buyer. Most e-commerce web sites like eBay do not allow the seller to shift risk of loss to the buyer until the seller completes delivery*).

DEPLOY to move forces to desired operations areas

DIRECTIVE military communication in which policy is established or a specific action is ordered; plan issued with a view to putting it into effect when so directed, or in the event that a stated contingency arises; any communication which initiates or governs action, conduct, or procedure

DISPATCHES military communications

DOG TAGS a soldier's personal identification

DOGS OF WAR allusion by William Shakespeare in his play *Julius Caesar*

DRAB (olive) shaded green color of the standard United States Military field uniform during World War II

GUERILLA GARAGE SALES

DRESS UNIFORM decorative attire required to be worn by all military officers on appropriate formal and ceremonial occasions

DUTCH AUCTION specific auction format in which multiple, identical items are listed for bidding [*Note: seller specifies the minimum price (the starting bid) per item, and the number (quantity) of items offered. Bidders bid at or above that minimum price per item for the quantity of items they are interested in purchasing. At the close of the auction, the highest bidders purchase the items at the lowest successful bid*].

FEEDBACK pioneered by eBay; a paperless trail of one's online reputation; a rating system that publishes to the world a user's overall business history, including such tangibles as the quality of goods, customer communication, payment history, service, and shipping; also a comment left by a registered user about their buying, selling, or trading experiences with another user; after a sale both parties to a transaction have an opportunity to rate their counterpart's business practices

FIELD EXPERIENCE proficiency resulting from encountering live exercises and actual combat

FLAK live combat fire directed at aircraft from the ground

FLYER taking a gamble or chance

FORCE a large contingent of military personnel, weapons systems, equipment and support, or any combination

FORWARD AREA an area near enemy contact

FORWARD OBSERVOR a soldier within visual range of artillery impact who reports the result and placement of rounds back to fire control

FRENCH UNDERGROUND term used for the resistance movement in occupied France opposing German Forces during World War II

GUERILLA a non regular combatant or irregular force

CASH HOFFMAN

GOVERNMENT ISSUE goods of unremarkable quality provided by the military to its personnel

GRADING system to distinguish and rank various items of a similar group or type of property to determine their physical condition and ultimately fair value

GROUND ZERO the location or point of round detonation and impact

HALF.COM an eBay company employing "fixed prices by design" with a strong following that remain loyal for that reason; an innovative site to buy and sell new, and pre-owned music, books, CD's, video games, movies, and other items at discount prices (as opposed to the eBay auction format)

HALFTRACK armored personnel vehicle with band tracks in the rear steered by front wheels

HANGAR large shelter usually suited for housing or repairing aircraft.

HOME PACKING during an estate sale a seller may include its inventory or offer several smaller estates together to make one sale without disclosing this fact to the public

HTML (Short for HyperText Markup Language) computer language used for creating World Wide Web pages; a block of text can be surrounded with tags that indicate how it should appear on the finished product (for example, in bold face or italics)

HUMVEE (High Mobility Multipurpose Wheeled Vehicle) modern highly durable light military motor vehicle that replaced the Jeep; also called a Hummer

HOWITZER a high powered artillery piece capable of high-angle fire

HQ Headquarters

HUMMER *see Humvee*

GUERILLA GARAGE SALES

INDIGENOUS FRIENDLY local non-combatant civilians that can be recruited for support

INTEL information that has been analyzed and evaluated to support tactical operations; the process of gathering strategic information

INTELLIGENCE processing enemy data, weather, and terrain impacting operations

INTERDICT disruption of enemy forces before they can be massed against you

INTERMEDIATE situated or acting between two points, stages, things, persons, etc.; in the middle of something

JAG Judge Advocate General Corp (legal arm of the military)

JEEP One of the first small four-wheeled drive vehicles used by the Military during World War II to transport several troops, supplies, and ammunition

JUMPING THE BID Bid raise interfering with the bidding rhythm at a traditional auction by increasing the bid exponentially instead of the standard ten per cent incremental raise *(Note: this is a strategy to chill the bidding and drive away other potential bidders)*.

JOINT OPERATIONS a general term to describe military actions conducted by joint forces

K-9 canine or dog

KP stands for *kitchen patrol;* describes cooking, cleaning and housekeeping duties in the mess hall

239

CASH HOFFMAN

LANDMINES self-contained explosive device placed in and on the ground to disrupt the movement of enemy troops and vehicles and destroy them

LIBEL statements falsely written and published that damage the reputation of another *See defamation*

LOGISTICS science of planning and carrying out the movement and maintenance of forces; those aspects of military operations that deal with: design and development, acquisition, storage, movement, distribution, maintenance, evacuation, and disposition of materiel; movement, evacuation, and hospitalization of personnel; acquisition or construction, maintenance, operation, and disposition of facilities; and acquisition or furnishing of services.

MAP COORDINATES horizontal and vertical lines on a map to pinpoint positions

MARCHING ORDERS official orders from HQ to move on or depart

MARRIED QUARTERS separate base housing for married personnel and their dependents apart from the barracks

MATERIEL all items such as ships, airplanes, vehicles, weapons, ordinance and support equipment (excluding real property and installations) necessary to equip, operate, maintain, and support military activity

MEDAL decorations worn on service uniforms signifying heroism, deployments, branch, and service

MEDIA MAIL United States Postal Service mailing classification; a less expensive, but non-expedited, way to send books, printed matter, audio recordings, and other "media mail" with a delivery time of 5-8 business days

MERCENARY a soldier for hire not necessarily motivated by patriotism

GUERILLA GARAGE SALES

MESS HALL dining and kitchen operations; the place where meals are prepared and served

MINT CONDITION pristine or blue-ribbon condition; refers to an item being graded for sale that looks and operates like the day it was manufactured without any flaws or visible signs of wear; brand new, as good as the day it was made; *(Note: it is quite rare to find a piece that is truly in Mint Condition).*

MISSION a task and purpose clearly indicating the action to be taken and the reason therefore; a duty assigned to an individual or unit; dispatching of one or more aircraft to accomplish one particular task.

MONSOON annual weather phenomenon in the tropic and subtropics with long periods of almost daily thundershowers

MOTOR POOL fleet of vehicles for common use; location where vehicles are stored

MUNITIONS military supplies, usually weapons and ammunition

NINE O'CLOCK antiquated but effective low-tech method to visually locate targets and enemy aircraft relative to your position. *(Note: By imagining your location at all times as being in the center of a clock face, each increment of time indicates a specific spot on the horizon to scan for fast identification. If the wing commander yells out: "bandits at nine o'clock," this means enemy aircraft is flying directly at your position on your heading and altitude and their approach is on your immediate right at a ninety degree angle. Twelve o'clock would indicate that an item of interest is above and directly in front of you at a higher altitude heading straight toward your position, and so forth).*

OBSTACLE COURSE any natural or artificial barrier that has to be traversed during practice or training exercises

OBJECTIVE clearly defined, decisive, and attainable goals towards which every military operation should be directed; specific target of the

241

action taken *(Note: for example, a definite terrain feature, the seizure or holding of which is essential to the commander's plan, or, an enemy force or capability without regard to terrain features).*

ON STATION being on duty at any military or naval activity at a fixed location

ORDINANCE Explosives, chemicals, pyrotechnics, and similar stores, e.g., bombs, guns, ammunition, flares, smoke, or napalm

PATINA change in an object's surface resulting from natural aging due to wear and oxidation; an appearance or finish that has developed with age, wear and tear; a general term applied to collectibles and antiques referring to the change in an object's surface resulting from natural aging that enhances its appearance and value

PAYPAL eBay-owned, account-based system that lets anyone with an e-mail address securely send and receive online payments using their credit card or bank account and is fast becoming the most popular way to electronically pay for eBay auctions (not limited to eBay transactions); an inexpensive way for merchants to accept credit cards on their on-line storefronts instead of using a traditional payment gateway

PHISING criminal activity utilizing the Internet to fraudulently acquire sensitive information, such as PIN numbers, passwords, financial, and credit card information, by masquerading as a trustworthy person or business in what appears to be an official authorized electronic communication

PIXEL Short for *Picture Element,* a pixel is a single dot in a graphic image containing thousands and millions more arranged so close together in rows and columns they appear to the eye to be connected in creating an image

PLANNING calculating, or the giving (or receiving) of information; carrying out of a strategic, tactical, service, training, or administrative military mission in the process of carrying on combat, including movement, supply, attack, defense, and maneuvers needed to gain the objectives of any battle or campaign

GUERILLA GARAGE SALES

POINT OF PURCHASE the place where a product is purchased by the customer such as a retail outlet or a display case and the purchaser and seller are both present

POLICE to clean or straighten up an area

PREEMPTIVE STRIKE an offensive action taken by a force before the enemy can strike its position

PRIMARY TARGET an object of high military value

PROCUREMENT acquisition of goods, services, or supplies

PROTOCOL set of rules governing conduct; etiquette

PROVENANCE place of origin; derivation, proof of authenticity, past ownership or source from where something comes; location and time of manufacture, production or discovery, expert opinion, written and verbal records, and history of an item

PROXY BIDDING a confidential maximum bid to an online auction service's automated bidding system; *(Note: The system's electronic "proxy" will automatically increase the buyer's bid to maintain the high bid. The proxy bidding system will stop when it has won the auction or reached the maximum bid set by bidder in advance).*

QUARTERMASTER soldier responsible for the supply of materiel

RECON (short for reconnaissance) field observation of enemy elements and positions

RENDEZVOUS a pre-arranged meeting at a given time and location from which to begin an action or phase of an operation, or to which to return after an operation

REPEL to fight against; a dispersal maneuver to insert or withdraw forces

CASH HOFFMAN

RESERVE AUCTION auction in which the seller reserves the right to establish a reserve price, to accept or decline any and all bids or to withdraw the property at any time prior to the announcement of the completion of the sale by the auctioneer

ROUND a single unit of ammunition

RUBRIC a scoring guide used in subjective assessments

RULES OF ENGAGEMENT directives under which military forces will initiate or maintain combat with the enemy

SECONDARY TARGET alternative target of lower value that presents itself when the primary target is unattainable or has been destroyed

SELF-INSURANCE A form of risk management through which a firm assumes all or a part of its own losses

SHIPPING CONTRACT a shipping contract immediately transfers ownership of the goods to the buyer once they are delivered to the carrier. (*Note: In this instance, the carrier becomes the buyer's agent and the buyer bears the risk of loss*).

SLANDER words falsely spoken that damage the reputation of another *see defamation*

SMALL ARMS man portable, individual, and crew-served weapon systems used mainly against personnel and lightly armored or unarmored equipment

SNAFU acronym for Situation Normal—All Fouled Up—a tactical mistake, blunder; military equivalent of Murphy's Law

SUPPORT action of a force that aids, protects, complements, or sustains another force in accordance with a directive requiring such action; unit that helps another unit in battle; an element of a command that assists, protects, or supplies other forces in combat. *See also logistics*

GUERILLA GARAGE SALES

SPECIAL FORCES highly trained unit responsible for special reconnaissance, unconventional warfare and counterterrorism

STORES military supplies

STRATEGIC INITIATIVE taking decisive action to control the course of a military situation

TACTICAL necessary activities to accomplish a mission; methods of winning a small-scale conflict; the actual means used to gain a goal; the level of war at which battles and engagements are planned and executed to accomplish military objectives

TARGET OF OPPORTUNITY a target of value that appears or presents itself during an operation for which there has been no prior planning

TRAIL BLAZER pathfinder, pioneer

TWELVE O'CLOCK *see Nine O'clock*

WAY POINT designated point or series of points to facilitate movement